Finding Peace in Iraq

Joint Field Research on New Approaches to Peacebuilding in the Kurdistan Region

A collaboration of the Center for Global Affairs
at New York University's School of Continuing and Professional
Studies and the University of Duhok

Talia Hagerty
Thomas Hill
Editors

Center for Global Affairs ◆ New York, NY, USA

Center for Global Affairs
School of Continuing and Professional Studies
New York University
15 Barclay Street
New York, NY 10007

ISBN: 978-1-304-19051-2

Cover photo © Katarzyna Szutkowski

10 9 8 7 6 5 4 3 2 1

Contents

i   *Acknowledgements*

ii   *Preface*

vi   *Map of the Kurdistan Region of Iraq*

viii   *Introduction*

1   **Education in Duhok: A Public Good or a Private Tension?**

Colleen Creegan

17   **The Impact of Business and Investment on the Turkey-Kurdistan Relationship: A Case Study of Duhok**

Lili Nikolova

37   **Downstream and Dismissed? The Kurdistan Region of Iraq and a Drying Tigris: A Case Study of Three Villages**

Alex Munoz

57   **An Examination of Peacefulness in Iraqi Kurdistan through the Lens of Religious Conversions**

Barbara Augustin

75   **Ensuring Minority Rights with Reserved Seat Systems in Parliament: Perceptions from the Kurdistan Region and the Disputed Territories of Iraq**

Megan Yasenchak

93   **Perceptions and Realities of Women's Rights in the Kurdistan Region of Iraq: A Case Study of Akre Community**

Katarzyna Szutkowski

117   *Glossary*

Acknowledgements

This collection would not have been possible without the generous support of the United States Department of State, particularly the Cultural Affairs Office at the U.S. Embassy in Baghdad, which provided funding that allowed the Joint Research Seminar in Peacebuilding to become a reality. Special thanks are due to former cultural affairs officer Suzanne Bodoin and assistant cultural affairs officer Farah Chery-Medor, both of whom have worked tirelessly to support this effort.

The authors, researchers, and editors who contributed to this volume owe a debt of gratitude to Dr. Vera Jelinek, divisional dean and director of the Center for Global Affairs (CGA) at New York University's School of Continuing and Professional Studies, whose visionary leadership created the space for this groundbreaking project to occur. Mark Galeotti, former academic chair of the CGA, also lobbied intensively on behalf of the project. And administrative assistant Anna Mosher made it possible for everyone to get where they were going – and to be comfortable once they got there.

Similarly, special thanks are due to Dr. Dawood Atrushi, vice president for international relations at the University of Duhok, who has made this partnership with NYU a special priority of his office. And finally, the contributors to this collection would be remiss if we did not mention the extraordinary contributions of Dr. Jotyar Sedeeq, the director of the University of Duhok's Center for Peace and Conflict Resolution Studies, whose dedication over the past decade has been largely responsible for the emergence of peace and conflict studies as a rigorous academic project at the University of Duhok.

Preface

A few months after the United States-led invasion of Iraq in 2003, the then-president of the University of Duhok, Dr. Asmat Khalid, first asked me when I would bring students from the United States to the Kurdistan Region of Iraq. He repeated the question to me many times in the years that followed, and usually I replied to him with a shrug of my shoulders and an explanation that universities in the U.S. were not eager to send students to any part of Iraq, a place known best for the unending images of violence that flashed across American television screens day and night throughout the first decade of the 21st century.

Dr. Asmat and I agreed, however, that bringing students from the U.S. to Duhok was a good idea, and that it could be an important and constructive step in the long process of repairing relationships between a generation of Americans and Iraqis who had known nothing but isolation and separation from each other due to dictatorship, war, sanctions and uninformed rhetoric in both of our countries. Dr. Asmat maintained that Americans needed to come to the Kurdistan Region, because once they did, they would realize that they had trustworthy friends in Iraq with whom they could work to build a better future and overcome misdeeds of the past. After more than 20 trips to Iraq – and the Kurdistan Region, in particular – to conduct research, and develop and deliver workshops and courses about peacebuilding, I could not have agreed more. One question remained: How would it ever be possible?

Less than two weeks after the U.S. had removed its last combat troops from Iraq at the end of 2011, I found myself at the U.S. Embassy in Baghdad, meeting with two cultural affairs officers and describing the ongoing partnership between our Center for Global Affairs at New York University's School of Continuing and Professional Studies and the University of Duhok. I told them about our just-completed joint project that had brought a group of Iraqi professors – including six from the University of Duhok – to New York to develop a master's level curriculum in peace and conflict studies. I spoke of my hope to create a new program that would enable graduate students from NYU and the University of

Duhok to work together on peace research projects. Less than two months later, the U.S. Department of State provided us with a grant to support the Joint Research Seminar in Peacebuilding. Suddenly, the Center for Global Affairs was in the business of incubating innovative research projects by graduate students at NYU and the University of Duhok. And for the first time in decades, a group of graduate students from the U.S. would be traveling to Iraq to conduct research with Iraqi counterparts.

The students' journey began in earnest late in July 2012, when seven students and recent graduates of the University of Duhok's Master of Arts in Peace and Conflict Resolution Studies arrived in New York and began the challenging task of negotiating research partnerships with nine NYU master's students: eight from the Master of Science in Global Affairs program and one from the Robert F. Wagner Graduate School of Public Service. Over time, three more representatives from the University of Duhok would join the group.

We spent two intense summer weeks talking together, exploring the notion of peace research, the types of projects that would be interesting and worthwhile, and mostly, trying to figure out how to accommodate the very different research interests that emerged from the students' very different life experiences. Adding to the degree of difficulty of an already complex project was the fact that neither university's team of researchers was anything close to monolithic. On the NYU side, we had eight women and one man, seven U.S. citizens, as well as students from Bulgaria and Indonesia, two vegetarians and one who had served in the U.S. Army in Iraq. On the University of Duhok side, we had eight men and two women, two working journalists, a former journalist, a former member of the Iraqi Parliament, and nine Muslims and one Yezidi. On both sides we had students ranging in age from their early 20s to their early 40s. We counted at one point that members of both groups spoke a combined 20 languages.

After research teams were established and project proposals were written, the University of Duhok group returned to the Kurdistan Region of Iraq. Over the months that followed, researchers from both universities corresponded by email, Facebook, and Skype to make sure that necessary arrangements were made for the NYU group's research visit to Duhok in January 2013. All of the proposals were vetted and cleared by the University Committee for Activities Involving Human Subjects at NYU.

We arrived in Iraq on January 3, 2013. Two members of the University of Duhok contingent met us in the wee hours at the Erbil International Airport and led a small caravan for the two-hour trip to Duhok, where we arrived just before dawn. As the NYU group waited for someone to open the university's beautiful new conference center where we would be staying, students marveled at the majesty of the surrounding mountains as they were revealed in early morning sunlight.

The next three weeks passed in a flash of field visits to refugee camps, interviews with government officials, political party representatives, businesspeople and religious figures, focus group meetings with students, long nights of reviewing and tabulating surveys, and constant discussions about what the next day would hold. Through it all, the NYU group was constantly amazed at the graciousness of our partners and hosts from Duhok, from the elaborate dinners to which we were invited to the simple and sincere daily expressions of concern for our comfort.

A week into our visit, a most unusual thing happened. Snow fell. It kept falling for an entire day until a foot of it blanketed Duhok – the heaviest snowfall the region had experienced in 20 years. The following morning, Dr. Asmat, now the Kurdistan Regional Government's Minister of Education, came to the university conference center to visit the NYU students. He reminded them that not every government minister would drive himself through the aftermath of a blizzard to visit a group of graduate students. Of course, he knew that this group was not just any group of students. It was the group he himself had invited to Duhok so many years earlier. Finally, a group of graduate students had made it to Duhok, to the Kurdistan Region, to Iraq, to work with their peers on peace research projects that would begin to fill the knowledge gap created by a generation of ignorance stretching halfway around the globe. It is my profound hope that the research presented on the pages that follow will be a step toward a time when students in the United States and the Kurdistan Region of

Iraq – indeed, all of Iraq – will find themselves engaged in such vigorous and constructive dialogue that they won't ever again allow their leaders to separate them.

Thomas Hill
New York, NY
July 2013

Map of the Kurdistan Region of Iraq

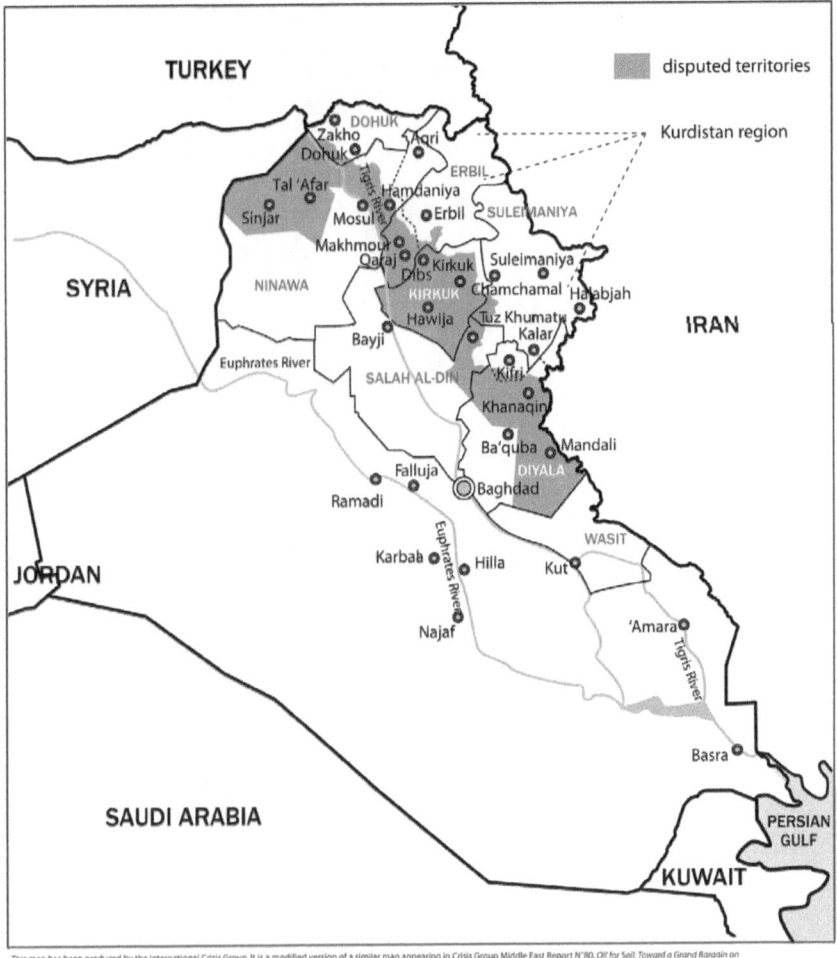

This map has been produced by the International Crisis Group. It is a modified version of a similar map appearing in Crisis Group Middle East Report N°80, Oil for Soil: Toward a Grand Bargain on Iraq and the Kurds (28 October 2008). Only the northern boundary of the disputed territories has been adjusted to add more detail.

Source: "Iraq and the Kurds: Trouble Along the Trigger Line." *International Crisis Group.* Middle East Report No. 88. 2009.

A note on place names: Translations from the Arabic and Kurdish languages to English often result in inconsistent spellings for place names in Iraq and the Kurdistan Region. As such, the spellings used in the map above do not all correspond directly with the Center for Global Affairs' preferred usage throughout the rest of this text. Dohuk, above, and Duhok, used throughout, refer to the same city, as do Aqri and Akre. Suleimaniya is the name of the same city and province referred to in the text as Sulaimani.

Introduction

The Kurdistan Region of Iraq (KRI) presents visitors – and its own inhabitants – with many contradictions. It is the only formal, political manifestation of the Kurdish people's deep and longstanding aspiration for a national homeland. It is also the direct consequence of a failed 1991 uprising that necessitated international protection against Iraq's former regime.

Home to as many as five million Kurds – as well as much smaller numbers of Assyrians, Turkmen, Arabs, and other minorities – the KRI is a place of great beauty: from the breathtaking Rowanduz Gorge and the nearby Gali Ali Beg waterfall to the ancient city of Amedi that sits atop a bluff and, on approach, appears to be floating in mid-air. It is also a place of great pain and sadness. The *Anfal* (Spoils of War) campaign carried out by Saddam Hussein's regime in the late 1980s resulted in the complete destruction of thousands of Kurdish villages and the forcible displacement of 1.5 million people (Marr 198-199). The 1988 chemical attack on the city of Halabja killed as many as 5,000 and left thousands more ill, disfigured and prone to birth defects (Marr 199; Bengio 181-183).

The very existence of the KRI is an anomaly caused by the confluence of historical events spanning the better part of a century. The post-World War I dissolution of the Ottoman Empire raised Kurdish hopes for an independent entity. In 1920, the Treaty of Sevres had envisioned an autonomous or independent Kurdistan. Indeed, the Kurdish leader Sheikh Mahmud Barzinji took steps toward establishing an independent Kurdish state in the early 1920's until he eventually fled from British forces into present-day Iran in 1924 (Marr 28-29; Tripp 54). Hopes for independence were relatively short-lived as the 1923 Treaty of Lausanne left the former Ottoman *wilayet* (provinces) of Baghdad, Basra, and Mosul – which contained most of the majority Kurdish areas – under British Mandate as the state of Iraq and the Kurdish population divided mainly between Turkey, Syria, and Iraq (Bengio 10-11).

Seven decades of tensions ensued between Iraq's largely Arab central government in Baghdad and various Kurdish factions based in the country's mountainous northern region. Contrary to popular belief, Iraq's Kurdish population was not always at odds with Baghdad. General Abd al-Karim Qasim, who led the July 1958 revolution that overthrew the Iraqi monarchy and led to the establishment of the Iraqi republic, sought to moderate ethnic and sectarian tensions, in part by appointing Kurds to significant government posts. The post-revolution provisional constitution referred to Arabs and Kurds as "partners ... within the Iraqi nation-state" (Davis 119). Qasim even invited Kurdish leader Mulla Mustafa Barzani back to Iraq from exile in the Soviet Union.

The honeymoon did not last. By August 1961, after Qasim had refused a demand for Kurdish autonomy, tribal groups in the north attacked the Iraqi Army, which responded by bombarding a village close to Barzani's headquarters (Marr 105-106). Qasim's rule came to an abrupt end in 1963 with a coup that included his execution, but the Kurdish struggle continued throughout the decade – culminating in a detailed 1970 autonomy agreement between Baghdad and the Kurds that called for Kurdish language rights, proportional representation in a future regional legislature and a national census that would determine areas of Kurdish majority (Bengio 50-57; Marr 152-153; Tripp 193).

Planned implementation of the agreement never took place, due to disagreements about the census and a 1971 assassination attempt against Barzani. By 1974, the two sides were fighting openly again. The Ba'ath government, which had taken power in 1968, had begun relocating Arabs to areas of Mosul and Kirkuk after deporting *faili* (Shi'a) Kurds to Iran (Bengio 57-60; Marr 152-153; Tripp 203-204). Barzani appealed directly to the United States, Iran and Israel for arms and aid (Marr 152; Bengio 69-78). Although it ebbed and flowed in response to national and regional political developments, the relationship between Iraq's Kurds and the central government did not improve throughout the decades that followed.

A major shift finally occurred in 1991. Following Saddam's 1990 invasion of Kuwait – and his subsequent loss to a United States-led coalition in the Persian Gulf War – the latest in a long series of Kurdish uprisings took place through the north of Iraq. As usual, the central government reasserted its control.

However, fears among the Kurdish population were higher than ever following the Anfal campaign and the attack on Halabja. Hundreds of thousands of people fled toward Iraq's borders with Turkey and Iran. The result was passage of United Nations Security Council Resolution 688, which called on Iraq to end repression of its own people and created the rationale for establishment of a no-fly zone north of the 36th parallel (just south of Erbil) patrolled by coalition forces, which forbade entrance by Iraqi aircraft (Bengio 197-204; Tripp 248-250).

The establishment of the northern safe haven enabled the mostly Kurdish population of the northern governorates of Erbil, Duhok and Sulaimani to create the Kurdistan Regional Government (KRG) in 1992. Among its first acts was to establish the University of Duhok. During its first 20 years of existence, the KRG gradually gained greater autonomy from Baghdad, a process accelerated by the 2003 U.S.-led invasion of Iraq that toppled Saddam's regime and the adoption of the 2005 Iraqi Constitution that formally recognized the right of autonomous regions to form and control many of their own affairs.

> ... [T]he Iraqi Kurds not only possess their most powerful regional government since the creation of Iraq ... but also play a very prominent role in the Iraqi government in Baghdad ... The actual division of power between the Iraqi government and the KRG, however, remains in potential dispute (Gunter & Romano 39-40).

The 2005 Constitution left open almost as many questions as it answered. Yes, the Kurdistan Region became a federally-recognized region of Iraq, but what exactly were its borders? Would the city or province of Kirkuk ultimately belong to it? And how, precisely, were natural resources – particularly oil and gas – to be developed?

These questions – and many others – are among the most contentious issues in the Kurdistan Region today. The question of so-called disputed territories tops the list. Article 140 of the Constitution calls for a census and a referendum to resolve the status of Kirkuk and other territories claimed by both the central government and the KRG. But the constitution did not define any process, and as of mid 2013, there had been neither a census nor a referendum and many communities continued to live under a sort of dual administration that, at times, amounted to very little administration at all.

Despite these political uncertainties, life goes on in the Kurdistan Region. Children attend schools, sometimes with two flags flying: one for Kurdistan and one for Iraq. Many young adults attend one of the region's 11 public and 10 private universities. Men and women work – still largely in the public sector, but also in agriculture, trade and, increasingly, in service provision. Young women, inspired in part by the KRG's 30-percent quota for female representation in the regional parliament, balance traditional social expectations against their own desires to play more visible and influential roles in public life.

The struggle for autonomy or independence that has dominated public discourse for so many decades has enveloped the Kurdistan Region in a veil of ethno-nationalism that can be seen in the omnipresent flag – a golden sun against three bands of red, white and green – that flaps atop almost every building. Also everywhere are large photos of the region's best-known leaders: Mulla Mustafa Barzani, who died in 1979; his son, Massoud, the current president of the region; Jalal Talabani, the president of Iraq; and Nechirvan Barzani, the prime minister of the KRG. The consistency of these images at times obscures the diversity of the KRI's population.

Although the majority of people in the region are Kurds and Sunni Muslims, there are significant concentrations of ethnic and religious minorities: Christians – representing the Assyrian Church of the East, Chaldean Catholic, Syrian Orthodox and Syrian Catholic churches – as well as Yezidis, whose most holy site, the Lalish temple, lies just outside Duhok. Turkmen, Armenians, Arabs, and Assyrians have significant minority populations in the region. Such religious and ethnic diversity – combined with past and current political conflict with the central government in Baghdad – combine to make the Kurdistan Region a fascinating crucible for the study of peace.

The papers in this collection are as much about peace research as they are about peacebuilding and peacefulness in the KRI. Not only do they examine particular issues of direct and structural violence in the region, but also the processes and challenges of exploring these issues with KRI residents and representatives. Some of the authors reached important conclusions about peacebuilding processes and offer distinct recommendations; others most clearly identified the next set of important peacebuilding questions. The first paper in this collection, "Education in Duhok: A Public Good Or a Private Tension?" forthrightly presents the challenges to validity and conflict sensitivity that are often unavoidable in this work. The project stands as a valuable example of the nuance of peacebuilding. This paper appears first in our collection because, although ultimately unable to answer the original research questions, author Colleen Creegan offers the reader a strong foundation in the region's context, the concepts of peace research, and structural violence.

Creegan touches on the conflict potential of scarce resources, and so her paper is appropriately followed by Lili Nikolova's study "The Impact of Business and Investment on the Turkey-Kurdistan Relationship: A Case Study of Duhok." This second paper addresses the imbalance that has developed in the economic relationship between the KRI and neighboring Turkey. Nikolova finds that, while courting economic development – a necessary component of peace – and international partnership, the KRG has privileged some Turkish citizens over its own. At the time of the study, Nikolova did not find this imbalance to be a critical conflict factor. In fact, the resulting economic growth seemed to be fostering a peaceful relationship between the KRI and Turkey and offering the KRI strength in its relationship with Iraq. However, with time, this economic imbalance may act as a barrier to fully realized structural peace.

Nikolova focuses on trade and the movement of mineral resources between the KRI and Turkey, but this is not the only resource challenge KRI citizens face. In "Downstream and Dismissed? The Kurdistan Region of Iraq and a Dying Tigris," Alex Munoz documents the dwindling water resources along the Tigris River and the effects of Turkey's upstream damming. With changes in water resources have come changes in relationships and social dynamics for Iraqi Kurds. Munoz finds that efforts to manage scarce water have been both a driver of conflict and a connector and capacity for peace. He highlights the necessary factors for peaceful water management, with sustainable development, vertical social capital, and broader structural peace being among them.

Beyond economic challenges, the KRI is also working to find the balance between social stability and diversity and individual freedom. Barbara Augustin's paper, "An Examination of Peacefulness in Iraqi Kurdistan through the Lens of Religion Conversions," explores one aspect of religion in maintaining family and social structures. Augustin finds religious conversion to be a source of social tension in Duhok and that changing one's religion is met with structural and/or direct violence. She observes a tolerance for religious diversity in the KRI, but this tolerance does not appear to permeate the family.

In the legal and political realm, religious and ethnic tolerance remains a challenge for the KRI, but one that society is working to address. Megan Yasenchak's study, "Ensuring Minority Rights with Reserved Seat Systems in Parliament," looks at the issue of minority political representation and the reserved seat system as a peacebuilding tool. She ultimately finds that the reserved seat system is not an ideal framework for building peace between religious and ethnic communities, but that it should be scaled up as an affirmative action policy to protect the rights of minority populations.

Finally, Katarzyna Szutkowski similarly examines a reserved seat system, as well as other policies and experiences in her paper "Perceptions and Realities of Women's Rights in the Kurdistan Region of Iraq: A Case Study of Akre Community." Szutkowski finds that, despite some recent progress, the female population of the KRI, and Akre specifically, still faces severe structural, cultural, and direct violence. Women represent half of the region's human resources, but are too often excluded from the processes of reconstruction and political and economic development. Gender relations remain an unresolved conflict in the KRI. Szutkowski presents a detailed account of the progress that has been made as well as the long road ahead in women's political participation, education, and freedom from violence and fear.

Each of the issues explored in these original studies

represents a single thread in the tapestry of relationships in the Kurdistan Region of Iraq that help to determine its contemporary level of peacefulness. Taken together, they offer a glimpse into the important historical, social, and economic dimensions of peacebuilding in the region's unique context. The editors, authors, and researchers who have contributed to this volume hope that these studies will contribute constructively to the important discussion of how to continue to build peace in the Kurdistan Region and throughout Iraq.

Works Cited

Bengio, Ofra. *The Kurds of Iraq: Building a State within a State*. Boulder: Lynne Rienner Publishers, Inc., 2012. Print.

Davis, Eric. *Memories of State: Politics, History, and Collective Identity in Modern Iraq*. Berkeley: University of California, 2005. Print.

Gunter, Michael M. *Kurds Ascending: The Evolving Solution to the Kurdish Problem in Iraq and Turkey*. Second Edition. Gordonsville, VA: Palgrave, 2011, Print.

Marr, Phebe. *The Modern History of Iraq*. Third Edition. Boulder: Westview, 2012. Print.

Tripp, Charles. *A History of Iraq*. Third Edition. Cambridge: Cambridge University, 2007. Print.

Education in Duhok: A Public Good or a Private Tension?

By Colleen Creegan

Research conducted by Sami Atroshi and Colleen Creegan

Abstract

As the fields of peacebuilding and peace research gain popularity and recognition, they continue to expand conceptually. No longer relegated to direct violence reduction, structural peace is becoming a key factor in what need be considered in order to build a peaceful society. Long thought of as a cornerstone of a functioning state, education has rightfully become a focal point of peace. Education intersects several aspects of the fields, as a mediation tool, a bonding site, and a means of measuring equality. Less research is dedicated to seeing how this resource could be a source of tension or division. This study was conceptualized as the two researchers explored the questions of how social service delivery in the post-violent conflict era of the Kurdistan Region of Iraq has the potential to rebuild trust and cohesion or fuel underlying tensions and resentments. As the maturing Kurdistan Regional Government learns how to govern and provide for its citizens, it has had to make decisions about the levels of international aid and support to accept. Social service supplementation, by external governments, NGOs, and private companies can influence a population positively or negatively. Here we will examine the impacts of the relatively new phenomenon of private schools in the researched region and how this dual supply track has impacted levels of perceived equality and peacefulness. In the end, our limited research did not provide us with concrete answers to our original research questions; however the process of conducting the research and examining the educational system through a peace studies lens has provided the field and us with dynamic leads on where further examination in the Kurdistan Region of Iraq should be conducted.

Introduction

> "Peacebuilding is the set of initiatives by diverse actors in
> government and civil society to address the root causes of
> violence and protect civilians before, during, and after violent
> conflict. Peacebuilders use communication, negotiation, and
> mediation instead of belligerence and violence to resolve
> conflicts. Effective peacebuilding is multi-faceted and adapted to
> each conflict environment. There is no one path to peace, but
> pathways are available in every conflict environment.
> Peacebuilders help belligerents find a path that will enable them
> to resolve their differences without bloodshed. The ultimate
> objective of peacebuilding is to reduce and eliminate the
> frequency and severity of violent conflict." – *Chic Dambach,
> former President & CEO, Alliance for Peacebuilding*

The reduction of direct violence and violent conflict has
typically been the basis of peacebuilding – what many people
understand as increasing negative peace. But the decrease in
indirect violence or social injustice is an equally key component in
achieving peace, known as increasing positive peace (Roberts).
Positive peace can involve a variety of structures, including but not
limited to: good governance, corruption reduction, minority
representation, free speech and media, and sufficient and equitable
social services. The widely expected forms of social services
provided by a government are health, education, protection or
security, infrastructure, and fair rule of law. These goods should
not only be provided, but also overseen and distributed in such a
way that all citizens, and non-citizens at times, have access to
them. For a developing or post-conflict country, with new leaders
and limited financial resources, providing adequate services often
can prove as difficult as maintaining a ceasefire.

Peace research, introduced in its modern form by Johan
Galtung's paper *Violence, Peace and Peace Research* in 1969,
preceded peacebuilding, which made its breakout UN appearance
in Secretary-General Boutros Boutros-Ghali's 1992 report *An
Agenda for Peace*.[1] Researching conflict at every stage provides

---

[1] Peacebuilding had been discussed academically since 1975 when Galtung
published his article "Three Approaches to Peace: Peacekeeping, peacemaking,
and peacebuilding."

peacebuilders with a nuanced understanding of peace attainment by challenging under-verified assumptions of the drivers of conflict. However, the act of and means by which qualitative research is conducted, especially within the framework of violence, needs to be examined. The social sciences, including anthropology, psychology, sociology, and now peace studies are widely criticized for their research methods, both by academics, and historically, by the populations being researched (Lather). In an effort to address the inequalities in access to and involvement in peace research, this study was designed to bring together an outside and an inside point of view.

Too often, western researchers with too little understanding of a situation spearhead research, relying on local residents as translators or supplemental researchers. Conversely, local researchers risk validity questioning based on personal experience biases or research agendas. Through a long-term collaboration between professors at the University of Duhok and New York University, a joint-research model was born that involved a local and foreign researcher to conceive, produce and study a research question pertaining to the Duhok governorate of Iraqi Kurdistan. Negotiating expectations, social norms, customs, and obstacles became as important to this project as many of the more common research pitfalls, such as asking the right types of questions within the right medium, protecting participants, and skewing data. Our findings addressed our original research question less than they shed light onto an area of peace research both ripe for further study and shadowed behind bureaucracy, mistrust, and uncertainty.

As my Kurdish counterpart returned to Iraq after our two-week seminar at NYU in August 2012, we had established a narrow and progressive set of research questions. The Kurdistan Region was becoming inundated with international tuition-based private school options, and we wondered how this new dual system was impacting tentatively peaceful interpersonal relationships within the city of Duhok, as some families were not able to afford private school. How were these schools affecting students' perceptions of themselves and their peers at alternate schools, in terms of their capabilities and levels of preparedness? How was this private competition influencing the choices for planning and strengthening the public school system by the regional Ministry of Education?

Examining the role of education in conflict as a potential driver and not only as a tool for reconciliation is a relatively unexplored area in the field. However, we believe that the questions continue to be valid. They are rooted in the framework of both traditional structural peace literatures, in addressing how classrooms function as microcosms of societies as a whole, and also in the widely accepted concept of resource allocation as a means of achieving structural peace. One of the unique and timely aspects for this research in the Kurdistan Region was the single public system that educated all students in the area until 2003 when the government opened its borders to allow in supplemental educational facilities. The schools that arrived were diverse in their background countries and teaching systems. Countries such as Iran, Turkey, England, and the USA established schools. Some schools were religious; others taught entirely in English. That these and other attributes that set apart these schools from the longstanding public schools had the potential to disrupt the cultural fabric of a newly defined region, still struggling with issues of identity, proved to be well worth investigating.

Context

Kurds, widely referred to the world's largest group of stateless people, are a non-Arab community that lives primarily throughout modern day Iraq, Turkey, Iran and Syria. Due to regional conflicts, both directly and indirectly involving the Kurdish people, many Middle Easterners of Kurdish decent have left the region and can be found in diaspora communities worldwide (O'Leary). Each of the state governments that control territory where large numbers of Kurds reside has a unique history with the Kurds within their borders. In this paper, we concentrate uniquely on the Kurdish Region of Iraq (KRI) and its citizens.

The semi-autonomous KRI is comprised of the three northernmost Iraqi governorates: Duhok, Erbil, and Sulaimani. It borders the rest of Iraq to the south and Iran to the east, Syria to the west, and Turkey to the west ("About the Kurdistan Regional Government"). The KRI and its inhabitants have fought for varying degrees of autonomy and full independence since the international inception of the state of Iraq in 1921. Persecuted by the Ba'athist regime that controlled the country from 1968 until 2003, Iraqi Kurds drew particular attention and support from many international actors after the genocidal attacks in the late 1980's, popularly referred to as Anfal (O'Leary). After a Kurdish uprising in 1991, the area was granted international protection by UN Security Council resolution 688 and became a "safe-haven" for Kurds. After the fall of Saddam Hussein, following the American-led invasion in 2003, Iraqis ratified a new constitution in 2005 that formally recognized the Kurdistan Regional Government (KRG) as the legal entity representing the autonomous Kurdistan Region of Iraq. The KRG continues to work in concert with the federal government in Baghdad ("About the Kurdistan Regional Government").

Two primary political parties control most of the power in the KRG: the Kurdistan Democratic Party (KDP) and the Patriotic Union of Kurdistan (PUK). There are also several smaller parties, such as Gorran, which garners most of its support from Sulaimani, and the Kurdistan Islamic Union (KIU), which presents the main source of political opposition to the KDP in Duhok. Erbil, the region's capital, is the primary home of the regional government. The presidency and parliament have been working on fair and accepted power sharing roles between their offices and parties to reflect the make-up and needs of their constituents. Respect for minorities' rights and fair representation have served as common ground for almost all the political actors in the region, most of whom remember all too well the suffering and underrepresentation they endured under the Ba'athist regime. The region is comprised of several different religious and ethnic groups, including a large majority of Muslim Kurds, and minority religions such as Yezidis and Christians, and minority ethnicities including Assyrians, Chaldeans, and Arabs, which vie for political positioning (O'Leary; Gunter & Yavuz). For the purposes of this paper, the lengthy and nuanced discussion of the make up of the KRG is less important than the recognition that the regional government is wholly and independently responsible for the educational decisions for the region. The regional government does, however, rely on the

Iraqi central government for most of its financial resources – a situation that has, at times, contributed to strained relations between the two governmental entities.

The KRG is outspokenly dedicated to improving the region's educational system independently from the rest of Iraq ("Education in Iraqi Kurdistan"). The KRG has received support from UNESCO and the World Bank, among other large donors, for the public schools' functionality and positive social impact. The region's mother tongue, Kurdish, has blossomed in classrooms as a show of regeneration and independence (Jamal). Not all public schools are consistent in their approach to utilizing Kurdish, Arabic, and English in classrooms, however, leaving the overall student body linguistically heterogeneous (Director General of Education Department – Duhok).

Currently, the typical student in a KRG-run public school will attend two years of pre-school, six years of required primary school, and six years of secondary school, which are divided into two three-year tracks ("Education in Iraqi Kurdistan"). While the government provides age recommendations for each stage, we found in our research that ages spanned several years by the time students reached the last two years of secondary school ("Education in Iraqi Kurdistan"). Public schools are mostly gender segregated, with boys and girls attending separate schools entirely. Private schools are more often mixed, with both genders sharing buildings and classrooms, but not always. Public school is free at every level, including university. However budgetary constraints coupled with the expectation to maintain a tuition-free environment have hindered the public school systems' growth and development. New buildings and maintenance on existing schoolhouses is one of the most pressing concerns for the KRG, parents, and students alike. Currently, to accommodate the number of students through the shortage of buildings, the government has installed a two-shift agenda. Standing public secondary school

---

[2] In our interview with the Headmaster of the public school, he stated that his school housed three shifts, but the third was an adult learning program and so does not count towards the regular system in our estimation. The evening program was overseen by a different headmaster and had a different curriculum altogether.

buildings throughout the region will house two separate cohorts in one day for three and half hours of instruction each, in comparisons to the full seven or eight hours that the private school students receive (Waladbagi; Public School Headmaster).[2]

Conceptual Framework

Education is impacted by violent conflict in a variety of ways, but can also serve to prevent further conflict. Children living in active conflicts zones suffer from poor access to, unreliable consistency, and instability of education. Often, in longer conflicts, funds for education may be diverted to arms and defense (UNICEF). Peacebuilding has welcomed a partnership with education as a means of reconciliation and conflict prevention. Classic examples include joint classrooms for members of groups in conflict or previously segregated communities. The idea that introducing ideas of inclusion and acceptance at a young age could play a major role in healing longstanding hatreds has permeated the peace-through-education field. Other frequently recognized benefits of continued education in times of violent conflict and in the immediate aftermath include its contribution to increasing social capital, the strengthening of state institutions, and the overall social benefits of strong and equal education (Godwin, Ausbrooks, & Martinez; UNICEF; "UNICEF – Evaluation Database – 2011 Global").

The well-documented, direct relationship between increased emphasis on education and levels of peacefulness is an important one, but it represents only one possible dimension of the relationship between peace and education. Our research examines the possibility of diversified educational options leading to higher levels of societal tension. We conceptualized education as a highly sought after resource. Uneven resource allocation always possesses the potential to cause disharmony. Research has been conducted in practically every country in the world about how finite resource provisions affect communities (Coulson; Dronkers & Robert; Godwin, Ausbrooks, & Martinez). Against the backdrop of the overarching theme of how education as a resource is allocated in the Kurdistan Region, we strove to pinpoint how a new dual-delivery system may have impacted the population's perceptions of educational equality and its effects on the community, if any.

For a richer understanding of how developing countries are utilizing private education successfully and otherwise, the work of Riddell and her comparative study of the effectiveness of public and private schools provided us with a framework for examining the new two-track system in the KRI. Her research concludes that efficiency – the number of students attending school for the lowest cost – is often at odds with effectiveness – the value of the education students are receiving. Though a system may be efficient, without proper oversight, either governmental or private, it is not guaranteed to be effective. However, more students with greater accesses to even subpar education, in and of itself is an accomplishment (Riddell).

Methodology

Our study focused on Duhok, the largest city in the governorate of the same name. Approximately 470 km north of Baghdad, the city is home to an estimated 350,000 inhabitants. The city is experiencing a boom in construction and trade, and hopes to capitalize on tourism due to its proximity to Turkey (The University of Duhok). We conducted research at two schools, one public and one private, which resembled each other in as many key aspects as possible. My co-researcher, Sami Atroshi, a student in the Master of Arts program in Peace and Conflict Resolution Studies at the University of Duhok, identified the two schools and introduced our research to the appropriate gatekeepers, who provided us with access to the schools. The schools chosen were two all-boys schools that are judged by Atroshi to be neither the top or lowest tiered schools but instead schools that would reflect the experiences of most students in either system.

The project was originally conceived in New York as a mixed methods study. Drawing from Joseph A. Maxwell's thinking about mixed methods research, we concluded that using questionnaires in addition to interviews and observations would provide us with complementary data sources (102). Following the common yet important practice of ethical oversight in social science research, in our case provided by NYU's Committee on

Activities Including Human Subjects, we had to take extra care to protect and respect our participants under the age of 18. For this reason we decided develop and distribute an anonymous questionnaire in order to minimize any possibility of exposing or exacerbating feelings of tension or resentment. The questions were co-written in English and translated to Kurmanji Kurdish for the public school students by Atroshi. The students in the private school received English questionnaires, and responded in kind. In the field, we also conducted one focus group in English at a third school, a private mixed-gender merit-based school, for a deeper understanding of the student's perceptions, however this data was used only confirm or contradict our primary findings.

For teachers and administrators, we created a set of open-ended questions to help us conduct guided interviews, and then asked appropriate follow-up questions. The interviews were held in English when possible, depending on the comfort level of the interviewee and when needed conducted in Kurdish or Arabic and later translated by Atroshi. Lastly, we met with the Minister of Education of Duhok and both the western and eastern directors of education, both for proper approval and simple interview questions.

Due to several unforeseen obstacles, some of our planned methods had to be altered in the field. The process of obtaining the proper levels of approval took longer than anticipated, which delayed our access to both schools. We also were confined by the fact that our research window coincided with the city's final examinations schedule, making classroom observation impossible. For this reason, we had to distribute our student questionnaires via the headmasters, which will be addressed in the validity section below. Sixty questionnaires were delivered to each headmaster. Thirty-four of the 60 were returned from the public school and 14 of the 60 were returned from the private school.

Data Presentation and Analysis

We found that this study did not successfully answer the research question because of the flaws in its design and methodology. After analyzing our data, I believe that we may have been too cautious with our questions and did not address the question of interpersonal conflict directly enough with our participants. The results of a differently designed study could be the same as the first one: that the schools have not created tensions. But I do not believe that this study alone provides us with strong enough data to confirm this apparent lack of increased tension.

The primary research question – Has the introduction of international private schools created interpersonal tensions between students within the city of Duhok? – could simply be answered "no," not according to any of the data we collected. No one in any of the interviews or returned questionnaires voiced any signals of conflict, violent or otherwise, between members of either system, or even fears of such conflicts occurring. Though the disparities between the two systems was very apparent to the participants, and mentioned often by them, there was a clear theme of personal choice or financial ability that dictated where students attended secondary school. Students addressed themes of fate, desire, parental influence, or proximity to their homes when discussing how they chose their schools. In terms of direct or interpersonal violence, it does not appear that the schools have the potential to increase or decrease it. The question remains, however, whether the disparities between the two systems are so great that they could be considered structural violence. Levels of expressed satisfaction and frustrations within both systems were similar enough that, for this sample, it would not appear that either group was or felt drastically marginalized.

However, the data collected is still engaging and relevant to peace studies. Because of the inconsistencies and looming validity questions, to be addressed below, attempts to code and reduce our data to conclusive findings proved less useful than analyzing the themes and outliers. Coding and statistical grouping offered questionable findings at best, because in every questionnaire we found contradictions. Consequently, it was impossible to measure individual participants' levels of contentment or displeasure. However, there were reoccurring themes that addressed issues not originally considered by the researchers.

The number-one feeling of injustice expressed at both schools studied, as well as the supplemental private school, was the testing system at the end of the 12th year, the final year of secondary school. All students are required to take final exams, their scores on which determine their eligibility and placement in higher education. The tests themselves were not the main concern to the students; rather they felt that the varied ways in which tests were administered and the rigidity of the scoring system posed significant problems. Students felt that some schools placed more emphasis on teaching 12th year students how to pass the tests than on simply educating them on the content of their curriculum. Other students expressed feelings of frustration with the cultural expectation that teachers who grade exams of family members or close friends will inflate those scores. Reference to paid after-school tutoring was also a reoccurring theme, suggesting an injustice for students who could not afford it. Themes of corruption and accusations that teachers withheld key information during regular class time in order to force paid tutoring peppered our data.

Students and teachers alike recognized the difference in class sizes and classroom time between the public and private institutions. Overall, student-to-teacher ratios were deemed appropriate at the private institution but classes were disproportionately large at the public school. Satisfaction levels with the infrastructure and amenities, such as laboratories and libraries, were higher at the private institution. Learning English as a primary language was also recognized as a benefit at the private institution. The majority of the students felt prepared for university, but several students at the public school credited themselves or outside influences more than the quality of instruction they received.

Instructional language was an issue addressed at every level as an obstacle, from the ministers down to the students. The academic language of Iraq is consistently Arabic, and the universities in the KRI follow this tradition. This causes conflict for the students from both the public and private schools, which are operated primarily in either Kurdish or English. Language influences many of the students' decisions about where to attend school, especially if they have the means to pursue an education at an international university. Honoring the ability to maintain Kurdish as an active academic language is important to the region as a whole, but the Ministry of Education should consider standardization of instructional languages.

Validity

> "That's bad science. While aid organizations must be accountable for outcomes, that pressure for positive results should not be an encouragement to skimp on the truth. Making a difference in the world is hard, often messy work. Pretending otherwise is no help at all." – *Sam Loewenberg, "Learning From Research Failure." The New York Times 1 Feb. 2013.*

This study has several problematic validity issues. Consistent and comparable sample sizes were not achieved. By not overseeing the distribution and collection of the students' surveys, we not only lost control of the numbers but also put the students in a position where they could not be certain that their answers were anonymous. Potential fears of their professors or headmasters reviewing their answers calls into question their ability to answer honestly and freely. For as much as we tried to protect research participants by the types of questions we asked and how they were worded, we did a disservice to the research and the participants by allowing individuals outside our team to handle and control the data. We also have no concrete knowledge of how the participants were selected. We asked the headmasters at each school to distribute the questionnaires randomly to students over the age of 16 in the 11th and 12th classes, but we did not define what we meant by the word "random." The public school surveys returned to us were only from the 11th class. We also have no guarantee that the questionnaires' responses were not read before being returned to us. Given the number of completed questionnaires that were not returned to us from either institution, it is feasible that those with certain types of answers may have been discarded.

Researcher identity also played a large role in our research. My Iraqi counterpart was an active political figure for several years, and is still widely recognized and identified as such despite his new role as a master's student at the University of Duhok. How the current ministers perceived him may have impacted the level of access we were granted to institutions and information. We repeatedly asked for citywide data on test scores and budget disbursement, but this data was never provided. It is also worth noting that the framework of peacebuilding and peace studies in education was often questioned, in terms of how it related to the current war in Iraq or the previous internal attacks on the KRI. We did our best to navigate these questions and explain the broader definition of peacebuilding, but we would be remiss not to acknowledge the sensitivity of the concept of peace and conflict for all of our participants.

Conclusion

Peace research continues to influence current thinking on the entire scope of global affairs. Understanding how violent conflict and structural violence impact the lives and development of humanity worldwide will help us create strong solutions for many of the dire hardships we continue to face. However, we cannot simply assert unverified assumptions about our thinking on attaining a peaceful world. We as researchers and activists must be willing to look at violence and peace with a critical eye and accept new thinking in this arena. With this in mind, our co-researched study on the role of the educational system in Duhok, Iraq, will add to the literature and field of peace studies despite its inconsistencies and data collection failures. We understand that the data collected may do little to answer our primary research question; it does, however, provide insight for future researchers into the realities of international field research, and particularly for research into the educational sector in Iraq.

From our limited research and observations, it does not seem to be the case that the new international schools are creating strain or resentment in the communities in the city of Duhok. We encourage further, more direct research in this area, as we merely skimmed the surface. What we did find was that students and administrators felt pressure and frustration with the inability of the public schools to meet the needs of the current student body in terms of infrastructure and teaching hours. Students in both systems also felt that the current secondary school exit exams created injustice and needed to be addressed governorate-wide in order to achieve equality. Further research in governance and oversight of the teachers would be welcomed by the community and provide even more data on how education and peace intersect in the Kurdistan Region of Iraq.

Works Cited

"About the Kurdistan Regional Government." *Kurdistan Regional Government.* Web. 21 May 2013.

Boutros-Ghali, Boutros. "An Agenda for Peace: Preventive Diplomacy, Peacemaking, and Peace-keeping." New York: United Nations, 1992.

Clarken, Rodney H. "Achieving Peace through Education." *ERIC.* 1986.Web. 22 May 2013.

Coulson, Andrew J. "Comparing Public, Private, and Market Schools: The International Evidence." *Journal of School Choice* 3.1 (2009): 31–54. Web. 23 May 2013.

Dambach, Chic. Qtd. in "What Is Peacebuilding?" *Alliance for Peacebuilding.* Web. 23 May 2013.

"Department of Foreign Relations Kurdistan Regional Government." *Kurdistan Regional Government.* Web. 2013.

Director General of education department-Duhok. In-Person Interview #3. Jan. 2013.

Dronkers, Jaap, and Peter Robert. "Differences in Scholastic Achievement of Public, Private Government-Dependent, and Private Independent Schools: A Cross-National Analysis." *Educational Policy* 22.4 (2008): 541–577. Web. 23 May 2013.

"Duhok City: Duhok the Most Peaceful Place All Over Iraq." *The University of Duhok.* 9 Apr. 2013. Web.

"Education in Iraqi Kurdistan." *Kurdistan Democratic Party-Iraq.* Web, 2013

Godwin, Kenneth, Carrie Ausbrooks, and Valerie Martinez. "Teaching Tolerance in Public and Private Schools." *Phi Delta Kappan* 82.7 (2001): 542–546. Print.

Gunter, Michael M., and M. Hakan Yavuz. "The Continuing Crisis in Iraqi Kurdistan." *Middle East Policy* 12.1 (2005): 122–133. Web. 21 May 2013.

Jamal, Randa. "Educational Reform in the Kurdistan Region of Iraq." *Reliefweb.* 19 Aug. 2008. Web.

Kingdon, Geeta. "The Quality and Efficiency of Private and Public Education: A Case-Study of Urban India." *Oxford Bulletin of Economics and Statistics* 58.1 (1996): 57–82. Web. 23 May 2013.

Lather, Patti. "Research as Praxis." *Harvard Educational Review* 56.3 (1986): 257–77. Print.

Loewenberg, Sam. "Learning From Research Failure." *The New York Times.* 1 Feb. 2013. Web. 22 May 2013.

16

Maxwell, Joseph A. *Qualitative Research Design: An Interactive Approach. 3rd Edition.* Los Angeles, CA: Sage Publications, 2013. Print.

"Nyange School." *Turikumwe! We're together!* Web. 23 May 2013.

O'Leary, Carole A. "The Kurds of Iraq: Recent History, Future Prospects." *Middle East Review of International Affairs,* 6.4 (2002): n. pag.

Private School Headmaster. In-Person Interview #2. Jan. 2013.

Private School Teacher. In-Person Interview #4. Jan. 2013.

Public School Headmaster. In-person Interview #??. Jan. 2013.

Public School Teacher. In-Person Interview #5. Jan. 2013.

Riddell, Abby R. "The Evidence on Public/private Educational Trade-offs in Developing Countries." *International Journal of Educational Development* 13.4 (1993): 373–386. Web. 3 May 2013.

Roberts, David. "Postconflict Statebuilding: From Negative to Positive Peace?" *Development and Change,* 39.4 (2008): 537-555. Web. 22 May 2013.

Skutnabb-Kangas, Tove, and Desmond Fernandes. "Kurds in Turkey and in (Iraqi) Kurdistan: A Comparison of Kurdish Educational Language Policy in Two Situations of Occupation." *Genocide Studies and Prevention* 3.1 (2008): 43–73. Web. 21 May 2013.

"The Kurdistan Region in Brief." *Kurdistan Regional Government.* Web. 22 May 2013.

The Role of Education in Peacebuilding: Literature Review. New York: UNICEF, 2011. Print.

UNICEF. *The Role of Education in Peacebuilding: Methodologiacl Framework for Three Country Case Studies.* New York: 2011.

Waladbagi, Salih. "Private Schools Increasing in Kurdistan Region." *The Kurdish Globe* 10 Feb. 2013. Web.

The Impact of Business and Investment on the Turkey-Kurdistan Relationship: A Case Study of Duhok

By Lili Nikolova

Research conducted by Lili Nikolova and Aram Balatay

Abstract

This study is a participatory action research project that seeks to answer the question: *How do citizens of the Kurdistan Region of Iraq (KRI) perceive the effect of the development of businesses between KRI and Turkey on their peaceful relationship?* The research intends to explain the balance of the positive and negative aspects of the economic interdependence for both Turkey and the KRI after the fall of the Saddam Hussein regime and the economic and political changes that came into effect in 2003. Based on the collected data, the report concludes that the economic interdependence between Turkey and the KRI certainly contributes to the achievement of a sustainable peaceful relationship between the two entities. However, this is more of a necessary component than a core factor. The economic relationship is also more beneficial for Turkey than for the KRI. The two major factors advancing Turkey in terms of profiting from the bilateral interdependence are the Investment Law of 2006, approved by the Kurdistan National Assembly, the parliament of the KRI, and the free visa regime for Turkish citizens in the KRI. While favoring Turkish businesses and entrepreneurs, these two factors serve as limitations for the local population and contribute to a lack of expected new employment opportunities and lack of capacity training and advancement of local industries.

Introduction

The main objective of this research project is to explore perspectives of citizens of the Kurdistan Region of Iraq (KRI) on how the development of businesses between Turkey and the KRI has affected the peaceful relationship between the two regions. This qualitative field study relied mainly upon interviews and personal observations conducted in Duhok, Iraq in January 2013. The interviews explored: the relative ease of attracting Turkish entrepreneurs and investments to Iraq; the longevity and sustainability of Turkish businesses in the KRI; fluctuations in unemployment rates; the effects of the Investment Law on new businesses; and how Turkish businesses have influenced the lives of citizens in the KRI.

Context

The lands between Duhok in the KRI and the city of Mosul, just 100 km to the south, have been contested territory for centuries ("Kurds protests Iraqi forces"). The Kurds are a distinct ethnic group without a state of their own. About 25 to 30 million Kurds live in the Middle East ("The Kurds"). The division of the Kurdish people among four modern states today – Iraq, Turkey, Syria and Iran – and their struggle for national rights have been constant themes of contemporary Middle Eastern history. The vast Kurdish territory was a part of the Ottoman Empire until its fall. When Kemal Ataturk ended the rule of the Turkish monarchy, Turkey, Iran, and Iraq each agreed not to recognize an independent Kurdish state. Kurds have struggled ever since to assert themselves in Iraq. More notably, throughout Saddam Hussein's regime (1979-2003), the Kurds, who form about 20 percent of Iraq's population, faced harsh repression and human rights violations that included widespread forced displacement and chemical weapon attacks ("The Kurds").

The United States' involvement with Iraq has led to the creation of a semi-autonomous region that is the closest entity to a Kurdish state since the end of World War I (Roy). The KRI is situated in northeastern Iraq, bordering Iran to the east, Turkey to the north, Syria to the west, and the rest of Iraq to the south.

Since 2003, the year of the Anglo-American intervention that overthrew Saddam's regime, major political, social, and economic changes took place in the KRI. Free from oppression from Iraq's central government and the economic limitations posed by international sanctions that had been imposed against all of Iraq following Saddam's invasion of Kuwait in 1991, the major priorities of the Kurdistan Regional Government (KRG) were to stabilize, economically liberalize, and democratize the entire region and work towards accomplishing economic growth, higher living standards, and peacefulness for its citizens. This shift involved privatizing Iraqi industries, creating a new currency, offering credit to Iraqi businesses, encouraging private entrepreneurship, rewriting the tax system, and lowering customs tariffs at border areas to facilitate open trade agreements (Roy).

In 2006, the KRG passed one of the most liberal investment laws of its kind in the Middle East. The law offered vast benefits for foreign investors, such as 10 years free of taxes once a business has started, access to reduced-priced land for investment, and rights to repatriate all profits, among other potential benefits ("Kurdistan's investment law"). As a result, commercial relations expanded rapidly with foreign businesses and regional states. By 2012, there were more than 1,200 Turkish companies in Iraq. More than half of them were located in the KRI, spanning many sectors: infrastructure development, wholesale, retail, investment, services, tourism, communications, and agriculture ("Nujaifi promises")

Turkey has a complex relationship with Iraq and the KRG. Relations between Ankara and the Iraqi Central Government in Bagdad were tense at the end of 2012. The Turkish Government had allied itself with the KRG and was engaging in successful bilateral trade centered on natural gas and oil extracted in the KRI (Mackey).

Complicating the picture, several Kurdish insurgent groups operate in Turkey, the largest one being the PKK, or, Kurdistan Worker's Party. PKK fighters often carry out violent attacks throughout Turkey, demanding greater recognition of political, cultural, and economic rights for Turkey's Kurdish population, as well as separation from Turkey and the establishment of an independent state of Kurdistan (Songun).

Despite this difficult issue, the economic relationship between Turkey and the KRI shifted in recent years towards stronger cooperation and partnerships for the purpose of mutual economic benefits. During the last few years KRI has supported the idea for a cease-fire between Turkey and the PKK. In 2012, Masoud Barzani, the President of the KRG, offered to mediate the conflict between the two sides to resolve the problem peacefully ("Massoud Barzani calls Turkey).

Methods

This study relies on data generated through 11 interviews and everyday observations of business and market activities in the KRI. Our research team interviewed four prominent KRG officials, two academics with expertise in political-economic development and marketing and innovations, and five business managers from Turkish-Lebanese-Iraqi companies. We also included data generated from informal conversations with four individuals who consult with construction and trading companies and two from non-governmental organizations. Not including the time for preparation and designing of the study, the data collection took twelve business days within a three-week timeframe during January 2013.

Data Presentation

This section contains the 11 questions asked in the interviews and a summary of the responses by all research participants:

I. *How has the KRI-Turkey economic relationship changed between 2003 and today?*

All interviewees agreed that after 2003 the economic relationship between the KRI and Turkey improved dramatically. Before 2003, the Kurdistan Region was described as closed and unsafe. The lack of safety combined with the hostile attitude of Saddam Hussein's regime toward any Turkish presence in Iraq were cited as the main factors that restrained Turkish companies from investing in the KRI. Kurdistan Region President Masoud

Barzani has been the key actor on the KRI side promoting partnerships with Turkey, as he has prioritized economic interests as key elements in all international relations (Interview 1; Int. 2; Int. 3). Barzani undertook policies promoting peace, reducing reliance on military solutions, and encouraging openness in the province, which have played a prominent role in attracting Turkey's interest in the region. He supported and approved the Kurdistan Investment Law of 2006 ("Kurdistan's investment law") and offered to mediate the conflict between the PKK fighters and the Ankara Government ("Massoud Barzani calls Turkey").

The KRI has been an autonomous region since 1991, but since the Iraqi Constitution of 2005 recognized the Kurdistan Region as a formal federal entity ("Timeline: Iraqi Kurds"), it has become easier for Turkish companies to negotiate and sign agreements within the legal framework of government agencies in the KRG without the need of approval from Baghdad.

Another radical driver of change in the quality of the relationship between the two regions was the Kurdistan Parliament's passage of the Investment Law of 2006, which led to a boost in the volume of bilateral trade. The KRI became a desired market for Turkish company products and a flourishing environment for Turkish investment. Turkey became the number-one buyer of the KRI's energy resources (Int. 5). In 2012, trade between Turkey and Iraqi Kurdistan amounted to $8 billion ("Iraq, Kurds, Turks and oil").

Turkish money has paid for building a new airport in Erbil, and for other large projects, due to growing demand for goods and services of all types: food products, clothes, building and construction materials, industrial goods, furniture, and electrical appliances ("Iraq, Kurds, Turks and oil").

II.   *Has the new Investment Law brought more employment opportunities to the Kurdistan region of Iraq?*

Generally, the interviewees agreed that due to the increased number of Turkish companies in the KRI, local residents of the region have more opportunities for work. However, the new jobs for locals are mainly in construction and infrastructure development sectors, and the openings are for low-skilled labor,

which has not helped the skilled resident workforce. The scarcity
of professional positions available for KRI residents in Turkish
companies is due to the fact that the latter prefer to bring their own
skilled personnel from Turkey (Int. 5; Int. 6).

The free visa policy for Turkish citizens in the KRI also
contributes to this dynamic. Visas for Turkish citizens in the KRI
are free and obtained upon arrival ("Visa Information"). Thus,
Turkish companies can bring workers of all skill levels – from
truck drivers to managers – into the KRI at very low cost (Int. 11).
The open visa rule gives the green light to the Turkish companies,
leaving others far behind. For example, there are many Lebanese
enterprises also interested in investing in the KRI and bringing
staff from Lebanon, but it is much harder from them since they are
required to have a visa to enter and work in the KRI (Int. 11).

Some of the interviewed company managers explained they
would prefer to hire local employees, but there is a capacity deficit
in the local workforce and a significant lack of expertise and
experience, especially technical skills, in the fields of business
management, engineering, and information technologies.

III.   Do you think the Investment Law threatens small local businesses?

The Investment Law has had a minimal negative effect on
small local businesses, as the regulation encourages the
development of activities that are new in the area. Most of the
Turkish businesses coming to the KRI have not taken over similar
local businesses since they were rare prior to the Turkish presence.
For example, there were only a few local private construction and
carpentry companies before the Turkish ones opened in the KRI.
However, some Turkish businesses have taken over small local
ones from their previous owners in the KRI. Examples include
retail stores, beauty salons, supermarkets, restaurants and cafes,
and fruit and vegetable markets. These cases have occurred not
because of the Investment Law, which require large initial capital
investment. Rather, it is the free visa program that makes it easy to
enter the semiautonomous region and open small Turkish
establishments with little capital, such as cafés, juice bars,
restaurants, home appliance shops, or clothing stores.

When walking along the streets of Duhok, one finds that most of the goods for sale are imported and almost all of them are from Turkey: cheese, clothes, ceramics, electronics, and many more. The various fruits and vegetables in the city bazaar also come from Turkey. Participants mentioned that they thought the Iraqi central government was responsible for this heavy importing because it did not allocate sufficient money to the KRG for investment in agriculture and for subsidies supporting local agricultural initiatives.

Some research participants said that the KRI is not a region that naturally develops entrepreneurs. The KRG employs many people in the public sector and pays relatively well. Therefore residents of the KRI are not generally motivated to take risks and the initiative needed to start small businesses (Int. 10; Int. 11).

IV.   *How easy it is for local government officials to attract Turkish entrepreneurs? What is the reason for the predominant presence of Turkish companies in the Kurdistan Region and Duhok?*

Research participants indicated that there were multiple factors enabling the presence of Turkish companies in Kurdistan.

Safety and Security

Not only the physical safety of the KRI, but also the safe investment environment and the promise of a high return on investment has attracted entrepreneurs. The major factor underlying this economic safety is the Investment Law, under which:

- Foreign and local investors and capital are treated equally under the law (Article 3)
- Foreign and local investors are entitled to own all the capital of any project (Article 3)
- The government allocates free or reduced-price land to investment projects that fulfill the criteria (Article 4)
- Foreign investors are free to repatriate profits in full (Article 7)
- Foreign and local investors are equally entitled to buy and own land for investment purposes (Article 4)

- Investors get a 10-year non-custom tax break once they start production or service provision. Raw materials and equipment used in production also get customs relief (Article 5) ("Kurdistan's investment law").

Geopolitics

Turkey's proximity to the Kurdistan Region has benefited Turkish businesses more than others. Turkey is conveniently located very close to the KRI and there are well-maintained roads between the two regions, facilitating the transportation of resources and materials across the border at low cost (Int. 11).

While a tense relationship exists between Turkey and the Iraqi Central Government, the KRG and the Turkish Government in Ankara are in a very close relationship due to the dependence of Turkey on natural resources extracted in the KRI. The Turkish government encourages Turkish companies to invest in the KRI, especially in the energy sector (Lee).

Large volumes of oil and gas have been transported unofficially from the KRI to Turkey, using road tankers, since 2003. Oil exported to Turkey has been used to meet the needs of energy-poor Turkey or has been refined into various products – plastics, heating oil, kerosene, synthetic fibers, and tires – before being shipped back to the KRI (Pamir).

In 2012, Ankara and the KRG declared a commitment to cooperatively construct pipelines to transport larger quantities of oil and gas (Kohen). The announcement worsened Ankara's relationship with Baghdad. Iraq's Prime Minister, Nouri al-Maliki, accused Turkey of wanting more than oil, stating, "Turkey made a deal with Iraq's Kurdish administration, and an agreement aimed to divide Iraq" (Kohen).

Overlapping cultural and social relationships

Most of the Turkish citizens involved in businesses in the KRI are from the southern part of Turkey, which is a predominantly Kurdish region. Thus, these Turkish citizens are ethnic Kurds who are familiar with the culture of life and business in the KRI, speak the Kurdish language, and feel welcome in the KRI – advantages Turkish companies enjoy compared to other foreign firms interested in the area (Int. 9).

*V.   Do you think the Turkey-Kurdistan economic
      interdependence has a positive, neutral or negative aspect
      for the KRI and how do you define that?*

Interview participants identified positive and negative aspects of the economic interdependence between the KRI and Turkey.

Positive Aspects

Turkish companies have been actively contributing to the reconstruction of KRI and infrastructure development – building roads, bridges, houses, apartment buildings, factories, offices, and other facilities. The Turkish enterprises provide social benefits for employees, such as healthcare plans and paid vacations. They also establish labor rights norms and regulations.

Interviewees emphasized the positive impact of Turkish business presence on political relations: the KRI needs to have a strong regional ally that is generally protected from external aggression. Turkey is unlikely to ally with Iraq's central government, or with KRI neighbors Syria and Iran. Turkey has given the KRI a gateway to Europe. It has been easy for citizens of the KRI to receive Turkish visas and travel to Turkey and from Turkey to Europe, especially for business events and conferences (Int. 2).

Negative Aspects

The KRI's industrial and agricultural sectors had decayed since Turkish companies offered better quality goods and services at lower prices. Therefore, there was a threat of the complete disappearance of local production and the private sector. In addition, the KRI residents with business education suffered from lack of employment opportunities and career training and development. In general, the KRI citizens were not motivated to start businesses, discouraged from the strong competition of the Turkish companies.

VI. *Do you think that economic interdependence leads to peace?*

Most participants hesitated or did not answer this question. Some said that economic interdependence could be a bridge to a peaceful relationship, as it generates mutual trust between the two parties. However, in this case, they were unwilling to say it would lead to peace because of the complicated political relationship between Turkey and the Central Government of Iraq and the tension caused by Kurdish insurgent groups in Turkey.

Turkey might be in a peaceful relationship with the KRG, but *de jure* the KRI is a part of Iraq, and the government in Baghdad supersedes the KRG; thus, a peaceful relationship between Turkey and the KRI depends on a peaceful political relationship between Turkey and the Central Government of Iraq.

Turkey might try to solve its problem with the Kurdish insurgent groups through the relationship it has with the KRI. In such a complicated political environment, research participants suggested that strongly intertwined economic ties were a necessary but insufficient condition for peace. However, such ties might play an important role in the process of achieving sustainable peace in the future.

VII. *Which kind of Turkish businesses are most important for a peaceful Turkey-KRI relationship?*

Most interviewees said that all businesses are important, but one person specifically pointed out the importance of construction businesses, which not only help to rebuild the region but also provide the most jobs for local KRI residents. The reasoning he offered was that the construction industry requires the involvement of many supporting sectors such as carpentry, masonry, and transport. And once new facilities are constructed, they require equipment and maintenance. Consequently, many other industries support the construction sector and benefit from it, resulting in a multiplier effect in terms of new jobs created for the local population.

VIII.   Do you consider this relationship friendly or solely based on economic needs? What are the social and political aspects of this relationship?

Most participants considered the relationship between Turkey and the KRI to be a business relationship based on needs but with strong socio-cultural and political aspects. For example, some Turkish companies had started establishing scientific and educational institutions to spread Turkish culture in the KRI. The role of shared religion – Islam and Islamic heritage – also heavily impacted the relationship between the parties. The interrelated past of the two regions has played a role in strengthening these ties.

As both regions used to be a part of the Ottoman Empire, the KRI and Turkey share a common historical and cultural background, which has significantly affected the nature of the relationship. Because of the similarities of culture, history, and religion, consumers from the KRI prefer Turkish goods and products to others (e.g. KRI citizens prefer Turkish food and clothes to European products). If Turkey had never been a part of the Ottoman Empire, or Christianity was the prevalent religion, the relationship with the KRI would not have been the same (Int. 4). Because of the close cultures, cases of intermarriages are common. As explained earlier, the majority of Turkish citizens working in the KRI are ethnic Kurds and so they often marry women from the KRI.

IX.   Can this relationship be the solution to the political tension between Turkey and the KRI?

Most of the interviewees believed that this relationship is not the entire solution, but definitely helps to lower the pressure. Turkish Kurds are known to have serious grievances regarding political, social, and cultural rights, but, according to the interviewees, the main reason Turkish Kurds are unhappy is because they are poor. In fact, economic disintegration is the prominent problem that triggers the other grievances. By sending Turkish Kurds to work in the KRI, Turkey has partially solved the economic side of the problem. Both high and low qualified Turkish Kurds are employed in the KRI. They are able to earn an income and use it to support their families back home. They spend the money in Turkey and thus the earnings from the KRI support the Turkish economy. This is another benefit for Turkey from the economic relationship.

X. *What do you wish you could change in the Turkey-KRI economic relationship and how would you like to change it?*

The interviewees pointed out the need for increased quality control for Turkish products and advancement of the technology sector in the KRI, so that the latter is able to produce competitive high quality goods. Related to that is the desire for capacity development in the province, to which not only Turkey but also other countries could contribute.

All participants would prefer a change in the balance of the relationship in favor of the KRI. If continued the way it is, the economy of the KRI will soon be subdued to the Turkish economy and this will threaten all local economic sectors with disappearance (Int. 4). The economic partnership is accepted as a successful experiment since the KRI needs the Turkish investments. However interviewees insisted that Turkish companies must pay taxes to the KRG (Int. 2). Lastly, it was mentioned that most Turkish companies work as contractors, not investors, and the KRI needs more investors instead.

XI. *How do you see the future of this relationship?*

Participants said that the relationship would keep prospering and the number of companies will increase; yet the scale of economic progress still depends on the political relationship between the Central Governments in Baghdad and Ankara because the KRI's economy is a part of Iraq's economy (Int. 3; Int. 4). Nonetheless, business between the two regions will keep growing regardless of the political tensions between KRG, Turkey, and The Central Government of Iraq. Participants felt that, because of the importance of the business relationship, none of these three entities will engage in violent conflict. Although The Central Government of Iraq is unhappy about the close ties between Turkey and the KRI, Iraq has a major stake in the energy trade and benefits even more than the KRI from the oil and gas exports from Northern Iraq (Int. 5; Int. 8; Int. 10; Int. 11).

Conceptual Framework & Data Analysis

We believe this study is a step forward in the exploration of innovative possibilities for building a peaceful relationship between Turkey and the KRI on the premise of mutual financial and economic gains. This study illustrates the conditions in 2012 for business and investment in the KRI, almost 10 years after the United Nations lifted most of the economic sanctions against Iraq. The significant reduction in sanctions resulted in the lowering of trade barriers and the opening of free markets. This article offers a report on the current economic environment in the KRI, and could serve as a resource for foreign companies and entrepreneurs who intend to invest in the KRI. It could also be utilized by the KRG to help reflect upon the region's current economic situation and needed policies, as well as by broader audiences interested in the KRI.

The analysis is embedded in three related and relevant texts that present concepts for a direct relationship between sustainable business and peace. Oliver F. William's edited collection *Peace Through Commerce: Responsible Corporate Citizenship and the Ideals of the United Nations Global Compact* addresses the purpose of corporations, the influence of legal and peace studies, the experience of career NGO officials and of business leaders, and how commerce can help promote peace. "*Peace Through Commerce (PTC)*" lays the groundwork for courses in business schools on corporate social responsibility, corporate citizenship, and the global environment of business, and presents the Matrix of Peace – a model based on the argument that successful commerce and development are both prerequisites for and contributors to sustainable peace (William 18).

The Matrix of Peace shows that peacefulness is more likely when robust marketplaces and a strong civil society intersect with functioning laws, structures, and institutions. According to this theory, when humans are engaged in their most basic and natural activities, one of which is participation in the marketplace, and the ground rules they follow are at the highest level of law and consciousness, then sustainable peace is a natural result (William).

According to this basic framework, all aspects of a successfully functioning, robust marketplace are present in the KRI – open and functioning free markets, private Iraqi industries, the modern Baghdad stock exchange, credit available to Iraqi businesses, booming private entrepreneurship, low customs tariffs, and flourishing international trade. In most of these economic activities, Turkey is a prominent actor. But is the involvement of Turkey in the KRI marketplace enough for the achievement of lasting peace?

The Investment Law is undoubtedly working in favor of Turkey, as explained earlier in the study, and is hindering the establishment and development of local KRI businesses. The free visa policy for Turkish citizens is an impediment to creating employment opportunities and developing local capacity and professional training for KRI citizens because Turkish companies prefer to bring employees from Turkey instead of training and hiring locals. The free visa regime also hurts small businesses such as restaurants, cafes, food markets, and retail stores. Turkish entrepreneurs can enter the KRI freely and develop small businesses, which do not require high initial capital. According to the Matrix of Peace, the KRI-Turkey economic relationship does not fulfill the requirement to contribute to sustainable peace.

In the text *Peace Economics: A Macroeconomic Primer for Violence-Afflicted States,* Jurgen Brauer and J.P. Dunne argue that creating sound economic policy and a stable macroeconomic framework is essential to societies recovering from violent conflict. Filling a gap in the literature on peace design from an economic perspective, *Peace Economics* extends beyond economic principles into the wider realm of social reconstitution, the social contract, and social capital in the hopes of helping practitioners build a more stable peace. The authors have combined general economic perspectives with case studies to explore economic growth in its broader aspects, while specifically stressing the role of internal and external conflict.

This analysis is based on the macroeconomic framework that a country should adopt to meet its economic growth and development goals. The framework consists of short-run economic stabilization, enabled by appropriate policy conditions, with the goals of long-run economic growth of assets, production, and income for long-run development and betterment of human life (Brauer & Dunne 16).

The data collected shows a fair presence of enabling policy conditions. The KRG has practiced transparent policymaking by passing the Investment Law and explicitly presenting its conditions and regulations. It has successfully implemented policy by embedding the Investment Law into the system of functioning laws and bringing it into action, which has attracted foreign investors to the KRI. These foreign investors were bound by the Investment Law and conducted business according to its rules. There were well-trained and accountable government officials – five of whom were participants in this study.

Where the enabling policy conditions have failed is in the regulatory framework. The regulatory framework of the Investment Law serves foreign investors well but it is not in favor of and does not protect local citizens and businesses. The free visa policy for Turkish citizens makes conducting business easier for them, but serves as an obstacle for skilled and unskilled residents of the KRI looking for jobs in the private sector.

These policy conditions have been able to achieve short-run economic stabilization in the KRI. There was low inflation in the KRI (until 2012, when the inflation rose to 5.6 percent ("Kurdistan Region-Iraq News in brief")), as well as free markets, a stable stock exchange, and a sound economic environment. The long-run economic growth of assets, production, and income for long-run development and betterment of human life is difficult to determine for this study. The KRI's economy has only been functioning freely for the past 10 years, which is a relatively short period of time, and the data we collected did not consist of information on growth of assets, production, and income.

In "Nation building and the role of the private sector as a political peace-builder," Julien Barbara explains the necessity of engaging the private sector as a peacebuilder in zones of violent conflict (581-594). He argues that the multinational private sector can make an important contribution to peacebuilding by using its influence as a key stakeholder. Current post-conflict state building approaches, such as those pursued in Iraq, have placed great emphasis on private sector economic activity as a basis for sustainable development (Barbara 581-594). These approaches have emphasized the importance of constructing accommodating post-conflict states capable of catalyzing private sector investment. The article also considers the role of the private sector as a political peacebuilder, and of how a failure to fully recognize the private sector as an inherently political actor may actually jeopardize the prospects for successful nation building.

This theory looks at Iraq as a state that has placed great efforts on private sector economic activity as a basis for sustainable development. Viewing the KRI using this approach, the region appears to have realized the importance of private sector investment, especially in the past few years, by attracting billions in investment from Turkey and utilizing the Turkish companies' engagement in the infrastructure sector to rebuild the region. In 2011, the volume of trade between Turkey and the KRI added up to $8 billion, which is the largest share in trade with Iraq as a whole ("Iraq, Kurds, Turks and oil").

At first sight the partners seem a good match: the KRI is energy rich but needs buyers and infrastructure and Turkey's rapidly growing economy needs energy resources ("Ankara to invest in oil").

Yet, in the case of Iraq, Barbara provides a simple reality check on the dangers of placing too much emphasis on the private sector's economic role and its contribution to peace and stability. He is concerned with the prioritization of private sector interests over those of other social groups and how this can exacerbate local tensions. His concerns seem justified as the relations between Baghdad and Ankara turned tense when the Iraqi government accused Turkey of interfering in its internal affairs ("Ankara to invest in oil").

The data from the conducted interviews also showed Barbara's concerns became a reality in the KRI. Interviewees expressed fear of losing job opportunities for KRI residents to Turkish citizens, as KRI residents lack professional training for specific industries, such as technology, and have poor capacity in general. Turkish companies could weaken the capacities of the local economy, and especially threaten the development of local agriculture and small businesses.

The second tenet of a successful private sector as a mechanism to promote peacefulness is using it for achieving political peace through track-two diplomacy by participating, for example, in policy discussions and negotiations with local stakeholders. In the situation of the KRI, there is an ambiguity about the effect of private sector efforts on political peace. The recent close economic and political ties between the KRI and Turkey have increased tensions between Baghdad and the KRG and between Baghdad and Ankara, especially since the official agreement of the KRG and Ankara to build oil and gas pipelines to transport larger quantities of energy resources. Prime Minister Al-Maliki has said that Turkey's greed for energy resources from the KRI will encourage the division between the KRG and Baghdad (Pamir).

This analysis shows that both the KRI and the KRG now face serious challenges after privileging the pure capitalist interests of the private sector over the interests and needs of the KRI citizens. The Turkish presence in the private sector has an unbalanced influence on the achievement of political peace since it positively affects the process of achieving political peace between the KRI and Turkey. However, it has some negative consequences on achieving the same between the KRI and the rest of Iraq.

Conclusion & Recommendations

The economic interdependence between Turkey and the KRI is a bridge to achieving a sustainable peaceful relationship between the two entities. Due to the complicated political environment and the dynamics of the multilateral political relationships between the Baghdad Central Government, the KRG, and the Turkish Government, the strong economic ties themselves are a necessary component but not sufficient for a peaceful relationship. Based on the data and the analytical framework, this relationship is more beneficial for Turkey than it is for the KRI. Laws that regulate the functioning of the private sector in the KRI, especially the Investment Law of 2006 and the free visa regime, favor Turkish businesses and entrepreneurs at the expense of the KRI's local population. KRI residents were unhappy with the lack of capacity training and technical development they have received, and the few skilled employment opportunities that have emerged for KRI citizens. They were also concerned about threats to small local businesses and the agriculture sector. The KRG has to maintain the flourishing of business and investment in the KRI, but at the same time, it has to create more benefits for the local population.

The KRG might consider:

- A budget for development and innovation in the KRI agricultural sector and programs for subsidizing local citizens who want to invest in the sector.
- Discussing amendments on the Investment Law to create more employment opportunities for citizens of the KRI (e.g. Turkish companies can bring personnel from Turkey but they have to be required to hire certain percentages from the local workforce).
- Investing in capacity training, especially in the technology sector, to raise the competitiveness of professionals and industries from the KRI.
- Making microloans available to entrepreneurs and small local businesses.

This conclusion does not underestimate the role of Turkey as a political ally and economic partner of the KRI, but rather seeks to explain the balance of positive and negative aspects – and the true possibilities for this economic relationship to contribute to increased peacefulness in the region.

Works Cited

"Ankara to invest in oil and housing field in Iraqi Kurdistan: Turkish analyst." *Kurd Net.* 9 Jan. 2013. Web. 24 Jun. 2013.

Barbara, Julien. "Nation building and the role of the private sector as a political peace-builder." *Conflict Security and Development*, 6.4 (2006): 581-594. Print.

Brauer, Jurgen and J. P. Dunne. *Peace Economics: A Macroeconomic Primer for Violence-Afflicted States.* Washington, D.C.: United States Institute of Peace, 2012. Print.

Interview 1-11. Personal Archive. Jan. 2013. Available upon request.

"Iraq, Kurds, Turks and oil: A tortuous triangle." *The Economist.* 22 Dec. 2012. Web. 20 May 2013.

Kohen, Sami. "Kurdistan Oil Pipeline would test Turkish policies on Iraq and Syria." *Al Monitor.* 24 Nov. 2010. Web. 20 May 2013.

"Kurdistan Region Investment Law." *Kurdistan Regional Government.* 25 Jun. 2010. Web. 20 May 2013.

"Kurdistan's investment law: The friendliest in the region." *Kurdistan Regional Government.* 25 June 2010. Web. 26 June 2013.

"Kurds protests Iraqi forces sent to disputed region on Syrian border." *Al Monitor.* 6 Aug. 2012. Web. 20 May 2013.

Lee, John. "Turkey encourages investment in Iraqi Kurdistan." *Iraq Business.* 7 Feb. 2013. Web. 27 Jun. 2013.

Mackey, P. "Iraq official fears split as Kurdish-Turkey oil trade grows." 19 Mar. 2013. Web. 18 May 2013.

"Massoud Barzani calls Turkey to release Ocalan and offers to mediate between it and PKK: Milliyet." *Kurd Net.* 14 Nov. 2012. Web. 20 May 2013.

"Nujaifi promises to ease Turkish investments in Iraq." *AlSumaria TV.* 5 May 2012. Web. 18 May 2013.

Pamir, N. "Turkey Contributes To Iraqi Fragmentation." *Al Monitor.* 20 Feb. 2013. Web. 26 June 2013.

"Visa Information." *Republic of Turkey Ministry of Foreign Affairs.* Web. 26 June 2013.

Roy, Sonia. *"The Impact on the Politics of Iraq and Turkey and Their Bilateral Relations Regarding Kurds Post-Saddam Hussein Regime.* Foreign Policy Journal." 22 Apr. 2011. Web. 20 May 2013.

Songun, S. "History of PKK in Turkey." *Hürriyet Daily News.* 9 Sept. 2009. Web. 26 June 2013.

"The Kurds (Iraqi Kurdistan)." *New York Times*. Web. 26 June 2013.

"Timeline: Iraqi Kurds." *BBC News*. 19 April 2011. Web. 18 May 2013.

William, Oliver F., ed. *Peace through Commerce: Responsible Corporate Citizenship and the Ideals of the United Nations Global Compact*. Notre Dame: University of Notre Dame, 2008. Print.

Downstream and Dismissed? The Kurdistan Region of Iraq and a Drying Tigris: A Case Study of Three Villages

By Alex Munoz

Research conducted by Alex Munoz and Shahnaz Zebary

Abstract

This paper is a qualitative study of the Kurdistan Region of Iraq (KRI) residents' views of peace and conflict and individual/group relationships and how they are impacted by increasing levels of water scarcity, especially with regard to the diminishing flows of the Tigris River. Utilizing 22 in-depth interviews in three different village areas, as well as interviews with government officials and university students, this study finds mixed results. Data generated illustrates both community resilience and connectors that support social cohesion as well as evidence of structural violence and dividers among some increasingly marginalized residents. All three cases point to a deficit in vertical capital between government and society, suggesting that expanded outreach from government officials could and should be undertaken in order to improve links between citizens and the state and to encourage a wider culture of sustainable economic growth that promotes long-term development and environmental and social sustainability in order to establish "peace as...healthy processes of change" (Ricigliano 17).

Introduction

According to the November 2012 post on website of the Iraqi Civil Society Solidarity Initiative,

> Once the cradle of civilizations, an agricultural haven…Iraq's land has dried significantly mostly due to man-made causes. For the past 20 years, upstream dams [on] the Euphrates have reduced Iraq's water income, and now the most important water lifeline in the country, the Tigris River, will be further reduced, having catastrophic effects on the lives of Iraqis who will see their livelihoods affected by increased drought and loss of lands due to lack of water (Iraqi Civil Society Solidarity Initiative).

Water scarcity in Iraq and the autonomous Kurdistan Region of Iraq (KRI) has only accelerated. A 2013 study announced that the Tigris and Euphrates river basins lost an amount of water equivalent to the Dead Sea from 2003 to 2009, as groundwater pumping became the common response to years of drought, drastically reducing groundwater supplies and endangering the future prospects of numerous communities in Iraq (Famiglietti).

The majority of peacebuilding research regarding water security has focused on interstate relations or examining situations after the outbreak of direct violence. Utilizing a more micro-level lens, this study examines the impact of water scarcity on KRI area residents' perceptions of peace and conflict and interpersonal and intergroup relationships, as well as community resilience, through a qualitative study conducted in three villages near the Tigris River.

Context

According to the United Nations Development Programme (UNDP), the Tigris River is forecast to lose approximately 80 percent of its year 2000 water discharge rate by 2025, predominantly as a result of sustained dam building upstream in Turkey (11). Turkey's Southwest Anatolia Project (GAP), especially its current project, the Ilisu Dam, which will greatly impact the flow of the Tigris River, has been met with widespread criticism and international attention (Finkel). However, "Turkey controls the Tigris and Euphrates headwaters...which dictates how much water flows downstream into Syria and Iraq" (Environmental Research Web), a situation complicated by the fact that "countries in the Tigris and Euphrates basins have not established a system to allocate water rights and jointly manage freshwater flows" (Morello).

Turkey's hegemonic control of "water flows into neighboring countries has already caused tension, such as during the 2007 drought, when Turkey continued to divert water to irrigate agricultural land" (Environmental Research Web). As reduced water flows heavily impacted northern Iraq, the area "had to switch to [pumping] groundwater" (Environmental Research Web). Elsewhere in Iraq, the central government responded to the situation of reduced water flow by drilling 1,000 new wells, an expansion of groundwater pumping that "has been the primary cause of recent groundwater depletion" (Martin).

If the Ilisu Dam, currently halted by Turkish courts (Dernegi), is completed, the Tigris River is expected to drop to less than half of current levels, from "from 20.9 billion cubic metres a year to 9.7 billion cubic metres" (Sands). This will likely lead to expanded reliance on new water wells, resulting in the further depletion of limited groundwater resources as populations compensate for the loss of surface water and thus increasing the impact of water scarcity. Water scarcity in the KRI has already resulted in "the erosion of livelihoods, decrease in crop production, increase in unemployment, and increase in some diseases such as typhoid and diarrhea" (UNDP 7). Area water scarcity has also affected rural migration patterns, "often accompanied by breakdowns in the integrity of communities and sometimes families," and sometimes resulting in "ethnic, family, or individual conflicts" (UNDP 11). If the Ilisu Dam is completed, it will dramatically impact individual and community relationships, likely exacerbating these conflicts.

Conceptual Framework

As originally conceived, this study posed the question:

How has water scarcity along the Tigris River impacted local residents' perceptions of peace and conflict and their individual and group relationships?

In framing this question, we hypothesized that increasing water scarcity resulting from a decreasing Tigris River and competition over shared water resources would negatively influence nearby residents' views of peace. Disrupted livelihoods and out-migration from the area were expected, as residents shifted from occupations tied to healthier conditions of the Tigris River – fishing and agriculture – and moved to the city of Duhok or elsewhere to seek new opportunities, leaving behind changed and fractured social networks. Residents' perceptions of Turkey, the country principally responsible for diminishing water sources through continued damming upstream, were expected to deteriorate. Opinions of Kurdistan Regional Government (KRG) and local government officials were also expected to have worsened as residents blamed government officials for declining conditions.

These assumptions were grounded in the United Nations Environmental Programme (UNEP) findings that the "collapse of livelihoods from environmental stresses, overuse of assets, or poor governance results in three main coping strategies: innovation, migration, and competition" (19). However, in arguing for a more systemic examination of environmental factors, UNEP also cautions that the environment and natural resources "are rarely, if ever, the sole cause of violent conflict. Ethnicity, adverse economic conditions, low levels of international trade, and conflict in neighboring countries are all significantly correlated as well" (8). "It is critical," urges UNEP, "that [environmental and natural resources issues] are not treated in isolation, but instead form an integral part of the analyses and assessments that guide peacebuilding" (19).

This holistic approach echoes the logic of systems thinking, which, according to Robert Ricigliano, "requires people to see the interconnections between distinct elements of a system, to see causality in dynamic rather than linear terms, and to look for patterns of behavior" (39). "Dynamic causality," in Ricigliano's words, "assumes that no initial conditions exists in isolation, rather that each is part of an interconnected system" (23), requiring an analysis that incorporates complexity and "stepping back from [individual] parts far enough to see patterns or wholes" (24).

UNEP additionally recognizes that while "environmental issues can contribute to violent conflict," the same environmental and natural resource issues can serve as "pathways for cooperation, transformation, and the consolidation of peace" (5). This dual nature of environmental issues, including water resources, demonstrates the concept of connectors and dividers outlined in Mary Anderson's *Do No Harm: How Aid Can Support Peace – Or War* (23-25). Similar to other connectors or dividers, water resources can intensify cooperation or competition between individuals or groups. Indeed, "today's dividers may be tomorrow's connectors" (76), prompting an examination of not just how water resources are viewed presently, but also the role they could play in the future if approached differently and under new conditions, especially increased scarcity. As individuals' relationships to water change, particularly in terms of access and allocation, water resources could shift from connector to divider or vice-versa, affecting the community context and, similar to aid flows, potentially "creat[ing] new sources of tension if care is not taken to identify divisions in the society" (75).

The connections between water scarcity and conflict are also the subject of Jason Gehrig's *Water and Conflict – Incorporating Peacebuilding into Water Development*. According to Gehrig, "scarcity of water and inequities in access, use, and decision-making can threaten life itself, diminish the quality of life, and impede integral human development" (v). Furthermore, "water scarcity is widely recognized as one of the causes of significant violence and conflict within nations" (11). Even in cases where direct violence does not occur, the "most widespread manifestation of water-related violence is the deprivation of access to improved water and basic sanitation, a situation of structural violence" (3). This expands on Johan Galtung's original concept of structural violence, which addresses constraints on human potential caused by economic, social or political structures (167-191). Tying the concept of structural violence to water scarcity also reflects that the conditions exacerbating the diminishing flow of the Tigris

River and the structural violence, manifest in inadequate access to drinking water, do not exist in a vacuum but result from political structures and decisions.

Structural violence, including water scarcity and especially if acting as a divider, will negatively affect levels of social capital – the "economic asset that consists of the social and communal networks that humans build" (Brauer & Dunne 13). Social capital represents "network[s] of mutual trust" and "a stock of achievements that…can be extremely difficult to rebuild" (Brauer & Dunne 13).

Two types of social capital exist: vertical social capital, which "represent[s] relationships and linkages between a controlling state and the society it controls" (Mahmoud, et al 47) and horizontal social capital, which typically is categorized as either bonding, increasing cohesion within groups, or bridging, linking across different identity groups (Putnam). Bridging capital and its resulting "networks of civic engagement that cut across social cleavages [and] nourish wider cooperation" (Putnam 175) have been linked to economic growth (Putnam 176). The idea that "violence is more likely where bonding social capital takes place at the expense of bridging social capital" (Mahmoud, et al 47) is crucial, especially given a context where water scarcity or another form of structural violence acts a divider, diminishing the capacity for the connections between groups that are necessary for bridging capital to flourish. "Social cohesion and peacefulness are more likely to occur where there is horizontal bridging capital and strong vertical capital" (Mahmoud, et al 64), an outcome that could be threatened by water scarcity functioning as a divider or where connections between the community and the state are weak.

More positively, the effects of water resources as a connector, thereby expanding bridging social capital, could be associated with improving social sustainability. The Institute for Economics and Peace defines social sustainability as "the strength of the social institutions that enable greater well-being and resilience ... enabl[ing] societies to withstand social, economic, political and environmental stresses, and shocks" ("2011 Discussion Paper" 43). Social sustainability has also been associated with "providing the social capital so that societies are more likely to pull together in times of difficulty than to fracture and fight" ("2011 Discussion Paper" 43). This corresponds with IEP's definition of resilience, the "capacity of social systems to absorb stress and repair themselves as well as a capacity for renewal and adaption" ("Structures of Peace" 5), and should be considered a pivotal aspect in examining the role of water scarcity and the diminishing Tigris River on local residents' perceptions of peace and conflict and individual and group relationships. Crucially, resilience, particularly the capacity to absorb stress, is a necessary component of Ricigliano's view of peace, "defined as achieving sustainable levels of human development and healthy processes of change" (17). Without adequate levels of resilience, social systems will not successfully and peacefully adapt to change and development.

Methodology

Aware of the limited time-span of three weeks in which to conduct site visits, we designed this project as a qualitative study. We began by utilizing a combination of Google Earth imagery and our local knowledge to limit the scope of our proposed research area, opting for villages near the Tigris River but north of Mosul Lake Dam. Initially, we considered selecting at least one village on the western bank of the Tigris River in Ninewa Province, but this option was later abandoned because security concerns connected to the violent conflict in Syria limited freedom of movement in such close proximity to the Iraq-Syria border. In discarding this possibility, logistical concerns were eased but the opportunity to incorporate perceptions and information from beyond Duhok Province was lost.

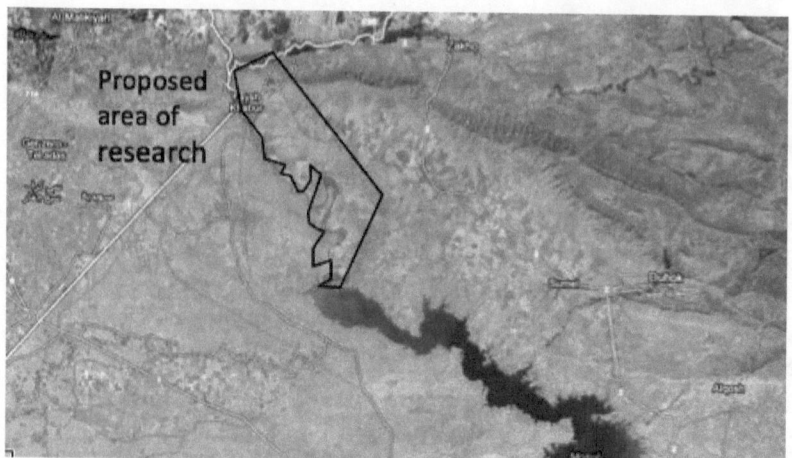

Imagery © 2012 TerraMetrics, Map data © 2012 Basarsoft, Google, GISreal, ORION-ME

Having established the general contours of a geographical area for examination, we next decided, in order to control for other variables, to select villages with members of different religious identity groups, including Christians, Muslims, and Yezidis, while also reflecting different socio-economic levels, including rates of land ownership. We opted for what Joseph Maxwell calls "purposeful selection" in choosing village areas, wherein "particular settings, persons, or activities are selected deliberately to provide information that is particularly relevant" to research questions in order to better test initial theories (98). Purposeful selection, especially in terms of designing this research as a three-village case study, allowed us to retain the "ability to elucidate local processes, meanings, and contextual influences" (99), while allowing for the opportunity to explore a "range of variation" (98) across different village communities.

Originally conceived of as the first sequence of study that would entail follow-up research, this project relied primarily on semi-structured in-depth interviews. The in-depth interview format allows researchers to guide conversations while "simultaneously leading the way with well-prepared, thought-through questions, and following the interviewee through active, reflective listening" (Hoglund 130). An interview guide was used to ensure that conversations began similarly and remained connected to questions of water security and perceptions of peace and conflict, but the semi-structured nature, wherein "each in-depth interview…take[s] different twists and turns and follow[s] its own winding path" (Hoglund 130), was considered ideal. This format allowed us to approach the context with a more open mind and to minimize and control our inherent biases and assumptions while allowing for the opportunity to explore important and related issues that a more structured format, such as surveying, could have overlooked. The added flexibility in the process allowed us to better examine selected villages more holistically, as per UNEP's recommendation that environmental and natural resources issues not be examined in isolation but instead be viewed in connection to other factors (19). Incorporating this open-minded flexibility also encouraged us to examine "the interconnections between distinct elements of the system" (Ricigliano 39) emphasized in systems thinking.

We viewed the capacity of in-depth interviews to assist in managing biases as a crucial aspect, reflective of the acknowledgement in our original research proposal that our own biases posed a threat to the validity of our study. UNEP, as previously mentioned, found that the three most probable reactions to the "collapse of livelihoods from environmental stresses…[are] innovation, migration, and competition" (19). And we recognized that the more semi-structured aspect of in-depth interviews offered the best format to control our biases so that more positive results, such as innovation, were not neglected.

We utilized convenience sampling. Considering that the villages we studied are small communities, we opted, when possible, to work initially through the local village leader, the *mokhtar*, recognizing that bypassing him and his position could be construed as disrespectful. Additionally, as respected village leaders, the *mokhtars* served as valuable gatekeepers to their communities and communal networks and working through such gatekeepers was seen as the "first step in grounding the research locally, for building rapport and trust, and for ensuring that the research questions make sense in that particular setting" (Hoglund, 134). Working with the *mokhtars* as research participants also acknowledged their role as key people, emblematic of their status as "important entry points" into and as influencers within their communities (Anderson & Olson 48). Cooperating with the *mokhtars* assured access to village residents, but we also worked to interview individuals beyond merely those suggested by the *mokhars* in order to ensure a better balance of viewpoints.

As the Tigris River and its diminishing levels have impacts far beyond nearby villages, we also sought to incorporate additional interviews in order to ground our study in a wider context. To this end, we contacted students and professors at the University of Duhok, as well as government officials, particularly from ministries involved with water usage and allocation, in order to better understand government attitudes and perceptions of water issues along the Tigris River. At all times, confidentiality was offered and maintained. In order to sustain this promise, individuals' names and the names of villages are not used in this paper, reflective of the reality that naming a village and that we had spoken with a *mokhtar* there would, essentially, identify the individual. In accordance with ethical practice, informed consent was established in all recorded interactions and we remained transparent in our university affiliations.

We had originally planned to use Google Earth imagery from several years prior in order to spark and facilitate discussion. However, this proved unnecessary. Despite an unusually snowy and rainy winter in Duhok, it was immediately and visibly apparent that the Tigris River was substantially lower than in previous years, as reflected in the below photos taken by the research team. Research participants were more than willing to point out nearby examples that illustrated the diminishing of the Tigris River.

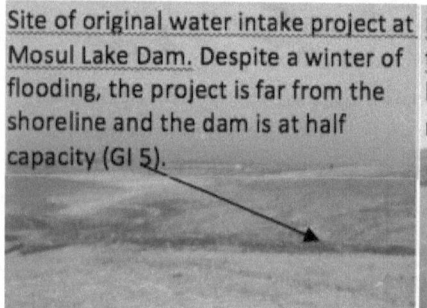
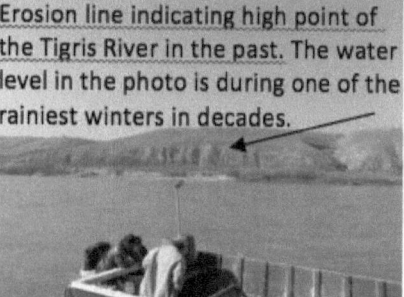

Site of original water intake project at Mosul Lake Dam. Despite a winter of flooding, the project is far from the shoreline and the dam is at half capacity (GI 5).

Erosion line indicating high point of the Tigris River in the past. The water level in the photo is during one of the rainiest winters in decades.

Presentation of Data

In accordance with our declared efforts to maintain confidentiality, data generated from interviews and site visits were individually coded. Juliet Corbin and Anselm Strauss' suggested steps for data analysis, as outlined in Jane Lawson's *What Happens After the War? How Refugee Camp Peace Programmes Contribute to Post-Conflict Peacebuilding Strategies*, were utilized, wherein, following individual coding, data was coded together by area, and then analyzed for "themes, variables, and subcategories" (5). Once coded, "interconnections were made between themes…form[ing] a story of the connections" (Lawson 5). Ongoing coding and analysis allowed for the refinement of "themes, categories, and their relationships as more data was gathered" (Lawson 5), maintaining a reflective process that also allowed for challenges to initial assumptions and the identification of gaps in knowledge. Research participants' comments will be identified with a reference code, according to the table below, with numbers corresponding to individual participants. For example, SI3 will refer to the interview with the third research participant in the community designated as Village Se.

Table 1: Total In-Depth Interview Participants

Location	No. of Interviews	Reference Code
Village Yek	5	YI + (1 − 5)
Village Dua	4	DI + (1 − 4)
Village Se	4	SI + (1 − 4)
Government	5	GI + (1 − 5)
University	4	UI + (1 − 4)

Village Areas in Brief

Village Yek was closest to the city of Duhok of our three selected areas and received regular piped water from the Duhok water system (YI1). However, area residents complained that, although they had sufficient water supplies for cooking, washing, and drinking, they did not understand why a recent change had dramatically increased their fees for water usage from 1,000 Iraqi Dinar to 10,000 Iraqi Dinar per month (YI3). This price increase generated bitter and frustrated comments (YI3). Another interviewee noted that residents were landless tenant farmers that came to Village Yek after fleeing violence elsewhere in Iraq and were hard-pressed to manage the additional monthly cost (YI4), their economic challenges and limited opportunities emblematic of structural violence.

Area residents seemed well aware of the Ilisu Dam and expressed grave concern they "[would] lose a lot of water" (YI2), and remarked that "the water of the Tigris River here is our life" (YI3). Residents speculated that if the Ilisu Dam were to be completed, "the Tigris River will go down and we will go back fifty years – everything will change" (YI2). Out-migration from the area was noted, as "young people cannot find jobs" (YI1) and frustrated fishermen regularly engaged in a form of asset stripping – depleting scarce assets to serve current needs (Brauer & Dunne 13) – by selling off fishing supplies, boats, and other items in order to fund survival and the ability to move elsewhere (YI2, YI 3). Perceptions of Turkey seemed unchanged, but there was the widespread view that Turkey would trade water for Iraqi oil (YI1, YI2, YI4, YI5), mirrored in interviews elsewhere (YD1, YD2, UI1, UI2, UI3). However, this positive view of interstate relations is tempered by individual concerns – "we always worry about the future" (YI2) – especially among those still working as fishermen. In addition to concerns over the Tigris River, fishermen expressed anxiety over fishing areas they shared with Arab residents on the far side of Mosul Dam Lake (YI2). In essence, they viewed such fishing areas as scarce resources to be competed over – a divider – providing support for UNEP's assessment that innovation, competition, and migration are the most common reactions to resource scarcity and affected livelihoods (19).

Villages Dua and Se, both located north of Duhok and near the border with Turkey, represented more positive portraits of conditions along the Tigris River. Well-maintained local homes and expansive and healthy farmlands suggested that these villages were more affluent than Village Yek (Field Notes). The *mokhtars* of both villages communicated with each other regularly, facilitating interactions between villages, while serving as valuable connectors who helped to promote peaceful relations (DI1, SI1). This connection was also facilitated by the fact that both villages depended on a shared underground spring for agricultural irrigation (DI1, YI2), a source that was viewed as reliable despite years of drought (SI3). Usage of the shared spring remained limited, though, as its high salinity levels rendered it unsuitable for drinking (SI2). Its high salinity has also harmed some crops irrigated by its waters (SI3).

Residents of both villages expressed general optimism for the future (DI2, DI3, SI3, SI4), remarking that "life is better than before – animals were used to plow the fields when we were children and now we use tractors, fertilizer, and have electricity" (SI2). This may relate to aspects of societal resilience, the idea that "higher per capita income implies a better functioning social contract, institutions, and state capacity," and that "economic development…diminishes motives for conflict" (Brauer & Dunne 113). Although residents expressed concerns over changes to the Tigris River, acknowledging that the Tigris River of their childhood years was "very different and clear enough to drink" (SI3), they expressed confidence that Turkey would make the right choice in using the river (DI4).

Research participants in both villages expressed confusion over why, after five years of promises and delay, they had seen no real KRG progress on initiating a proposed water project nearby that would result in purifying their shared spring so that it would be suitable for drinking (DI1, DI 2, D3, DI4, SI1, SI2, SI3, SI4). Despite this frustration, none of the residents interviewed articulated any feelings of anger with the government. Their statements and actions so far exemplified the moderating effects of local economic development (Brauer & Dunne 113). The lack of drinking water was mentioned as the greatest problem for both villages (DI2, SI3) and all residents interviewed mentioned the necessity of buying drinking water. However, despite the frustration with the cost of purchasing drinking water for their families, especially during the hotter summer months, residents felt they made sufficient income from agriculture to cover these costs (SI2, DI3). Out-migration was commented on as limited (SI1, DI4), but individuals also expressed that many younger people had not returned to the area when the population moved back following the United States' invasion and the fall of Saddam Hussein (SI3, DI2), having instead opted to remain in their newer homes elsewhere.

Data Analysis

Theme: Different Trends, Different Perceptions

In the course of our research in each of the three selected village areas, we found mixed evidence to support our initial assumptions accompanying our research question. Instead of encountering only signs of communal breakdown and fractured social networks, exacerbated by water scarcity, as seen in Village Yek, we also encountered examples of community resilience and adaption in Villages Dua and Se. Fundamentally, both contrasting examples – Villages Dua and Se's resilience and Yek's eroding sense of community – differed in their overall trends, the "relatively durable dynamics and patterns that influence developments" (USAID 31). Trends, according to USAID, can include "contextual factors" such as the "environment, economic changes, [and] demographics" (31). In all three villages, environmental factors were deteriorating, particularly as impacted by the diminishing Tigris River and increasing water scarcity. But for Villages Dua and Se, the positive economic trend, according to residents, outweighed the environmental factor of water scarcity.

For Villages Dua and Se, the majority of residents also benefited from the shared experience of largely being returnees who had been able to come back to their family lands after years of displacement caused by Saddam Hussein's regime (SI3, DI2), a narrative that served as a connector between villages and individuals. However, the opposite experience was more common in Village Yek, as residents largely had fled violence and instability elsewhere in Iraq following the U.S. invasion (YI4), only to encounter uncertain economic and environmental conditions. For Village Yek, the result has been a vicious cycle, wherein more pessimistic views of the future were shaped by negative environmental and economic factors (YI1), prompting asset stripping and out-migration (YI2), weakening the existing social bonds as people move away, undermining local resiliency, and contributing to a deepening pessimism regarding the future. "Once these cycles are underway they can be self-reinforcing and very difficult to reverse" ("Structures of Peace" 5), which indicated a continuing negative trend for the remaining residents of Village Yek.

Theme: Innovation and Resiliency – KRG and Local

KRG officials contacted were unanimous in their view that current water conditions throughout Duhok governorate were sustainable and they indicated that villages suffering from severe water scarcity received assistance from the government, including via the trucking of water supplies to some remote villages (GI3). The KRI, as a whole, was viewed as more adaptable to the changing conditions of the Tigris than the rest of Iraq, as most of the KRI benefits from underground aquifers that are renewed by rainfall and ice melt (GI1). However, officials also acknowledged that if the Ilisu Dam is completed, "the Tigris River will be dry in five years" (GI3). This would be a potentially severe shock to residents of the KRI, especially the most vulnerable populations already suffering from structural violence, such as residents of Village Yek.

Water wells and the Duhok water system are regularly monitored to measure cleanliness, salinity, and other factors (GI1, GI5). KRG officials expressed concern with ensuring that water supplies remain sustainable for the KRI's growing population, especially its urban areas (GI2), reflective of "sustainable economic growth [which]…must serve developmental purposes and be ecologically sustainable" (Brauer & Dunne 16). Part of ensuring this long-term sustainability is tied to charging more for water supplied by Duhok's water system (GI5). These price increases are part of an effort to ensure that the costs of maintaining Duhok's water infrastructure can be properly maintained, and are a preliminary step towards measuring and charging for water usage through the implementation of water metering systems in order to limit demand and consumption (GI5). This sort of planning, while intended to mitigate the risk of greater water scarcity, can be viewed as a form of choice architecture, "the self-conscious and deliberate design of incentives that inhibit undesired and promote desired individual behavior, such that a social system as a whole moves toward a desired outcome" (Brauer & Dunne 142), particularly toward reduced tensions and increased peacefulness. In this case, water metering, by tempering consumption and increasing long-term sustainability, can help reduce water scarcity and resulting competition.

On the more local level, Village Dua represented another intriguing example of resiliency, as, according to interviewees, the community has assisted poorer residents in buying tractors, fertilizer, and other agricultural supplies by pooling financial capital through the utilization of existing networks of social capital (DI1, DI4). The collaboration between *mokhtars*, the shared historical narrative of returning home, a tradition of peaceful coexistence between different identity groups and the mutual use of a local spring for agricultural water all serve as connectors that function as capacities for peace, "individuals and institutions [that] maintain intergroup peace" (Collaborative for Development Action 3). These connectors added to the level of resiliency within Villages Dua and Se.

Theme: Information as Issue – Vertical Capital Deficit and Recommended Action

Vertical social capital, which includes "relationships and linkages between a controlling state and the society it controls" (Mahmoud, et al 47), was lacking in all three village areas. This deficit was reflected by the confusion and frustration over water price increases in Village Yek (YI3), which had weakened the already-loose connection between poorer, marginalized area residents and the government, souring their perceptions of government capacity. As "social cohesion and peacefulness are more likely to occur where there is horizontal bridging capital and strong vertical capital" (Mahmoud, et al 64), the KRG should work to expand vertical capital networks between government agencies and isolated rural communities that have experienced structural violence, especially poorer areas, such as Village Yek. Residents of Village Yek expressed aggravation that no reason was given for recent price increases even when government representatives came to collect monthly water fees (YI2). Should area residents continue to feel detached from government polices as a result of weak vertical capital, they may feel that their participation in the social contract, the "framework of widely agreed upon rules of social cohesion and trust, along with external or self-policing enforcing institutions" (Brauer & Dunne 112), is no longer valued, likely undermining trust and increasing tensions and conflict.

In the course of interviewing university students with regards to vertical capital (UI1, UI2), it was suggested that this deficit be addressed by working through existing institutions, particularly local schools, that could serve to better channel information from government agencies to area residents and potentially encourage environmental responsibility (UI1). This shift would "change the interconnections between elements within the system" (Ricigliano 38), utilizing area schools to act as enablers of vertical capital while attempting to encourage long-term shifts in student attitudes in order to promote environmental awareness and sustainable economic growth and away from culture that "wastes everything," including water (UI1). University students also recommended that expanded government ties be used to encourage information regarding more efficient forms of irrigation (UI4), a crucial area where government support could disseminate both information and distribute useful existing technology (Famiglietti, 2013).

Conclusion

Our three-village case study cannot be generalized across Iraq or along the Tigris, but it does support UNEP's assertion that reactions to environmental factors often vary between migration, innovation, and competition. The KRG, through its efforts towards long-term water management, including water metering in order to promote sustainability, appeared to be bolstering levels of resilience. Improving economic trends also seemed to be overshadowing environmental factors, including water scarcity, in some cases. Yet even in the most positive cases, there appeared to be a deficit of vertical capital connecting the government with the governed. Addressing this shortage of vertical capital offers a potential pathway toward not only connecting communities with the government, which would increase social cohesion, but offering information that could help change attitudes and behaviors towards long-term environmental sustainability and economic development, grounded in a view of peace "defined as achieving sustainable levels of development and healthy processes of change" (Ricigliano 17).

Works Cited

Anderson, Mary. *Do No Harm: How Aid Can Support Peace – or War.* Boulder, Co: Lynne Rienner Publishers, 1999. Print.

———— and Lara Olson. *Confronting War: Critical Lessons for Peace Practitioners.* Cambridge, MA: The Collaborative for Development Action, 2003. Print.

Brauer, Jurgen and J. P. Dunne. *Peace Economics: A Macroeconomic Primer for Violence-afflicted States.* Washington, DC: United States Institute of Peace, 2012. Print.

Collaborative for Development Action (CDA). *The Do No Harm Handbook (The Framework for Analyzing the Impact of Assistance on Conflict).* Cambridge, MA: CDA Collaborative Learning Projects, 2004. Print.

Dernegi, Doga. "Controversial Ilisu Dam on Hasankeyf Halted by Turkish Court." *International Rivers Website.* 10 Jan. 2013. Web. 15 Feb. 2013.

Environmental Research Web. "Groundwater Levels Drop at 'Alarming' Rate in Large Swath of Middle East." 19 Feb. 2013. Web. 21 Feb. 2013.

Famiglietti, Jay. "Weighty Water Matters in the Middle East." *The National Geographic Website.* 22 Feb. 2013. Web. 22 Feb. 2013.

Finkel, Andrew. "Turkey's Ilisu Dam Should Not Be Built." *The New York Times.* 17 Feb. 2012. Web. 15 Feb. 2013.

Galtung, Johan. "Violence, Peace, and Peace Research" *Journal of Peace Research,* Vol. 6, No. 3 (1969): 167-191.

Gehrig, Jason, and Mark M. Rogers. *Water and Conflict – Incorporating Peacebuilding Into Water Development.* Baltimore, MD: Catholic Relief Services, 2009. Print.

Höglund, Kristine and Magnus Öberg. *Understanding Peace Research: Methods and Challenges.* New York, NY: Routledge, 2011. Print.

Institute for Economics and Peace (IEP). "Structures of Peace: Identifying What Leads to Peaceful Societies." Sydney, Australia, 2011. Print.

———— "2011 Discussion Paper: New Dimensions of Peace – Society, Economy, and the Media." Sydney, Australia, 2011. Print

Iraqi Civil Society Solidarity Initiative. "Impacts of Ilisu Dam in Iraq: A Lecture at the Marine Science Center Basra University." 28 Nov. 2012. Web. 15 Feb. 2013.

Lawson, Jane Elizabeth. "What happens after the war? How Refugee Camp Peace Programmes Contribute to Post-conflict Peacebuilding Strategies." New Issues in Refugee Research, United Nations High Commissioner for Refugees. Oct. 2012.Web. 26 Jan. 2013.

Mahmoud, Alia, Anupah Makoond, and Cherine Yassien. "How the Private Sector can Contribute to Peacefulness: A Three Country Case Study Analysis of Mauritius, Rwanda and Somalia." Center for Global Affairs, New York University, New York, NY: 2012. Print.

Martin, Claire. "Parched Middle East Faces Severe Water." *The Smithsonian Website.* 15 Feb. 2013. Web. 21 Feb. 2013.

Maxwell, Joseph A. *Qualitative Research Design: An Interactive Approach. 3rd Edition.* Los Angeles, CA: Sage Publications, 2013. Print.

Morello, Lauren. "NASA Probes Show 'Alarming' Water Loss in Middle East." *Climate Central Website.* 19 Feb. 2013. Web. 21 Feb. 2013.

Putnam, Robert D. *Making Democracy Work: Civic Traditions in Modern Italy.* Princeton, NJ: Princeton University Press, 1993. Print.

Ricigliano, Robert. *Making Peace Last: A Toolbox for Sustainable Peacebuilding.* Boulder, CO: Paradigm Publishers, 2012. Print.

Sands, Phil and Nazar Latif. "Iraq's New War Is a Fight for Water." *The National.* 4 Sept. 2009. Web. 15 Feb. 2013.

United Nations Development Programme. *Drought Impact Assessment, Recovery and Mitigation Framework and Regional Project Design in Kurdistan Region (KR).* Jan. 2011. Web. 15 Feb. 2013.

United Nations Environment Programme (UNEP), *From Conflict to Peacebuilding: The Role of Natural Resources and the Environment.* Nairobi, Kenya: United Nations Environment Programme, 2009. Web. 5 Jan. 2013

An Examination of Peacefulness in Iraqi Kurdistan Through the Lens of Religious Conversions

By Barbara Augustin

Research conducted by Barbara Augustin, Shilan Shawkat Almahmada, and Omed Mohamad Taher Muqdad

Abstract

The goal of this research is to examine the perception of peace held by those living in the Kurdistan Region of Iraq, using the lens of religious conversion. This endeavor was accomplished by applying the local definition of peace to explore how religious conversion positively or negatively impacted peace and society within Christian, Muslim and Yezidi communities living in Duhok. This work does not assume that religious conversion is negative or positive, but that it may impact levels of peacefulness. Any change to identity ultimately alters society. Those tensions, if exploited, could have broad and violent implications on peace and society in the Kurdistan Region of Iraq.

Introduction

Kurdistan is a region known as "The Land of the Kurds". The Kurds are the largest stateless minority in the world, with an estimated 30 million Kurds living in Turkey, Iraq, Iran, Syria and Armenia. (Roy 1) Both Iran and Iraq have political states that bear the name Kurdistan. This study took place in Duhok, located in the northern part of Iraq.

The Kurdistan Region of Iraq (KRI) has three governorates, governed by the Kurdistan Regional Government (KRG) and the Iraqi Central Government. Duhok is one of the eighteen provinces of the KRI and appears to be relatively peaceful. Compared to the rest of Iraq, bombings are few and security measures are effective (Phelps 457).

Despite Kurdistan's location and contentious relationships with the countries it spans, the region is ethnically and religiously diverse. "Kurds are largely Sunni Muslims, Indo-European speaking people. They are distinct ethnically from the Turks and Arabs, but are related to the Iranians" (Gunter 197). The countries that span the Kurdistan region have largely influenced Kurdish society and culture. "The Kurds notoriously are divided geographically, politically, linguistically, tribally and ideologically" (Gunter 198). Given this groups' diverse background, there are several religious beliefs and practices in the region. This study focuses primarily on religious affiliation within the three dominant religions in Iraqi Kurdistan: Islam, Christianity, and Yezidism.[1]

Religion is the cornerstone of society and cultural norms in the KRI. It maintains a dual role in identity and culture. This work does not assume that religious conversion is negative or positive, but espouses that it has the potential to disrupt the overall social fabric and may impact levels of peacefulness. Many Kurds assert that religious conversion does not occur, nor does it lead to violence. However, data gathered from our research team's

---

[1] The majority of Kurds are Sunni Muslims. There are also Shi'a Muslim and Yezidi Kurds, as well as Christians who identify themselves as Kurds. Yezidis are Kurds who follow a religion that combines indigenous pre-Islamic and Islamic traditions. The once-thriving Jewish Kurdish community in Iraq now consists of a few families in the Kurdish safe haven (O'Leary 2002).

interviews with two religious converts and acknowledgement from research participants that religious conversion occurs contradicts these claims. We found that the denial of the existence of religious conversions and violent reactions to conversions was based on a traditional definition of violence – primarily, physical violence[2]. Meanwhile this research found evidence of structural violence and psychological violence suffered by religious converts. Psychological violence can be as disruptive as physical violence. Any change to identity ultimately alters society and can lead to violence or foster tensions upon interpersonal and intergroup dynamics. Those tensions, if exploited, could have broad and violent implications on peace and society in the Kurdistan Region of Iraq.

Context

Religion is an extremely important part of the region's social fabric. It could be argued that religion undergirds the democratic principles of the region. Article I of the Iraqi constitution states that Iraq is a "federal, independent and fully sovereign state in which the system of government is republican, representative, parliamentary, and democratic." The preamble introduces and states the purpose of the constitution by beginning with, "in the name of God, the Most merciful... (Iraqi Constitution)" The preamble makes it clear that Iraq is deeply rooted in religious principles. Although the KRI is directly governed by the Kurdistan Regional Government (KRG), the region does not have its own constitution and falls under the purview of the Iraqi constitution and legal system, which is based in part on Sharia law.

Sharia law is followed in Iraq and the KRI as a function of the constitutional framework. "Conversions by Muslims to other faiths is forbidden under most interpretations of Sharia and converts are considered apostates (non-Muslims, however, are

---

[2] Although there are many types of and terms for violence, the phrase physical violence is used here because was the phrase used by Iraqi research participants. The examples they gave of this were suicide, murder, etc. Physical violence is akin to direct violence, and is used here to distinguish the violence in question from psychological, structural, or cultural violence.

allowed to convert into Islam)" (Beehner). Some Muslim clerics consider conversion from Islam to be a crime punishable by death. This legal precedent stretches back to the seventh century when the Prophet Mohammed ordered a Muslim man to death because he joined the enemies of Islam during a time of war (Beehner).

> In most Muslim states, matters of marriage, divorce, inheritance, and other personal-status areas are handled by Sharia courts, whose judges tend to be conservative. Sharia judges are usually educated in academic institutions which do not favor intellectual independence. They are taught "to memorize the Quran and the *hadith* (traditions related to words and deeds of Prophet Mohammed)...consequently, if there is a misinterpretation, they will simply automatically apply it (Beehner).

During the field research phase of this study, several individuals told our research team that the issue of religious conversions was not relevant to peace research. Some asserted that religious conversions did not take place in Duhok or elsewhere in the Kurdistan Region. However our team interviewed two converts and spoke with one who declined to participate in our research because of fear. This subject is a very sensitive topic for many reasons. Denials of religious conversions seem to result from the lack of legal evidence of these faith conversions. Since it is illegal to convert from Islam to other religions under Sharia law, it could be perceived that the acknowledgement of such conversions would mean complicity. A male and female research participant corroborated that conversion is not allowed in Islam. Furthermore, a convert we interviewed stated that when she converted, friends and family disowned her because of shame and the fear that they would appear to tolerate her conversion.

At the time of this study, there was not a consensus among the three main religions in Duhok about how religious conversions should be addressed.[3] There is, however, a shared definition of

---

[3] Yezidi religious leaders considered conversion punishable by death. Alternatively, Christian participants did not share any principles or laws stating that death is the penalty for religious conversion. These responses were collected in the field.

peace in the region. Many of the research participants defined peace as coexistence, harmony, respect for others and unity under the Kurdish nationality. A key component of this definition is that individuals remain in their religious groups. The concept of peace was closely tied to religious homogeneity. Although there were villages and towns inhabited by different religions, there were few inter-religious households or families. There appeared to be tolerance of religious difference in schools, work places, and communities, but diversity of religion within families is not reflected in the household. The family and household are two of the institutions where evidence of structural violence can exist.

Conceptual Framework

There is a dearth of existing research that specifically addresses how people in the Kurdistan Region of Iraq react to religious conversion. There are a small number of cases of religious conversions that involve physical violence, according to news articles and research interviews. For example, in 2007 Du'a Khalil Aswad, a 17-year old Iraqi Kurdish girl of the Yezidi faith, was stoned to death in an honor killing (Ekurd.net). Male members of her family allegedly killed her because she converted to Islam to marry a Sunni Muslim man (Ekurd.net). Although this case appears to be an extreme and perhaps isolated incident, there has not been significant research into the reactions to religious conversion in the Kurdistan Region of Iraq.

The closest case available for examination is the case of Iranians who sought asylum in Turkey following the 1979 Islamic Revolution. Consequently, we will use this case as a major part of the conceptual framework to help develop an understanding of religious conversion in Iraqi Kurdistan. Unable to travel to western countries, it is estimated that 500,000 to 1.5 million Iranian nationals used Turkey as a transit country (Fuller; Ghorashi; Icduygu; Akcapar 22). While in Turkey, 10,000 to 15,000 of the migrants converted from Islam to Christianity. Some of these converts changed their religious affiliations out of the belief that conversion could be their only way to reach the West (Akcapar 834), as Western countries and humanitarian relief agencies sometimes (possibly inadvertently) demonstrated partiality toward

Christian minorities. Other converts had more personal motivations, including the fact that they had practiced Christianity secretly in Iran, but once in Turkey, publicly pronounced their faith; others converted as a means of integration and assimilation.

> We became Christians 18 years ago. We were Shiites before. We were keeping our conversion as a secret in Iran. Then my eldest boy told one of his best friends in secrecy that we became Christians. There was persecution against Christians. When friends and neighbors learned that we converted, they started to call us "najes" (dirty). My children were discriminated at school because of their religion. My husband lost his work in one night as someone put the shop on fire. The firefighters could never find out the reason of the fire (Shirin, female, 35 years old) (Akcapar 835).

Johan Leman writes that religion functions as a(n):

- Institutional conveyor of (ethnocultural) bridging
- Medium of socio-cultural integration
- Medium for affirming original culture
- Celebration of cultural and religious syncretism
- Engine of (non-) adaptation (Akcapar 818).

This study relies upon Leman's proposition because it helps us understand the importance of religion in Kurdish life, especially as the large majority of Kurds are spread across five different countries and, thus, are subject to many different sets of cultural norms. Religion, thus, becomes a major cultural marker for many Kurds, who see it as a common identity trait they share that crosses national boundaries. This fact seems to be true both at the micro (family and social) level as well as at the national level.

Religious ethnocultural bridging appears to be threatened by conversion in Duhok. Conversion from one religion to another could be a form of ethnocultural bridging, but in this society, which is governed by Sharia law, conversion into Islam is the only legally acceptable form of conversion.

In addition to the case of Iranian religious converts in Turkey, this study draws on peacebuilding concepts such as structural violence – proximate and structural causes of violent conflict – to help explain how the strain on social relationships can result in violence after faith conversions occur. It addresses how change affects social identity and peace in Duhok. In order to comprehend the social triggers that contribute to religious violence, our research team needed to identify the types of violence (i.e. physical or non-physical), the profile of perpetrators or instigators of violent acts, and the underlying conflict dynamics. Then local peace capacities could be identified.

Methodology

This research was designed using a hybrid flexible model and took six months to complete. The methodology for this research involved three stages:

1. Desk research at New York University
2. Dield research in Duhok
3. A local impact analysis and preparation for dissemination of research results that occurred both in Duhok and New York

The hybrid flexible model included a needs assessment, a focus group, and individual and group interviews. According to Joseph Maxwell, a qualitative study cannot be logically strategized in advance and then implemented. Instead the research design should vacillate from construction to reconstruction, and our design allowed for this fluidity. For all forms of data generation, the research team attempted to obtain representation from Christians, Muslims, and Yezidis throughout the study. There were 43 participants in this study.

The desk research portion of the assessment took place in New York and was conducted primarily by the NYU student member of the research team from August to December 2012. The two University of Duhok researchers identified participants for the focus group and interviews, which were all conducted in Duhok in January 2013.

Phase I

Our research began with an exploration of Kurdish culture, history, and current events and religious conversion case studies in countries neighboring Iraq. The interview questionnaire (roughly eight to 10 questions were used to interview research participants) and informed consent forms (explicit explanation of the purpose of the study, identification of the researchers, as well as the expectations of the research participants and researchers) were drafted and written in English, then translated into Arabic and Kurdish. In addition to conducting background research and preparing documents used in the field, the needs assessment took place in September and October 2012.

The needs assessment was necessary to help determine whether the initial research goals were relevant to the research participants. Prior to delving into the question of whether religious conversions enhance or undermine peace within a society, it was important to first assess whether such conversions existed (i.e., Muslims to Christianity, Yezidis to Islam etc.).

The team conducted individual interviews with professionals (non-Kurdish and non-Iraqi) living abroad who possessed knowledge of religion and the KRI. The conversations identified issues of importance to the Kurdish people in Iraq.

Phase II

The second stage of research took place in Duhok in January 2013. Field research included a focus group composed of 14 students across ethnicities and religions: 8 males and 6 females from Duhok University. The focus group took place in one day during the first week of the field visit and lasted two hours. The participants were not compensated for their participation. All three researchers were present as facilitators. The session was audio recorded with the approval of the participants. The focus group participants were asked a combination of questions from the individual and needs assessment questionnaires.

We also conducted 27 individual interviews in six villages around Duhok. Interviews ranged from 15 to 60-minutes and were often conducted at the desired location of the research participant (e.g. court offices, classrooms, places of business, homes, etc.).

Group and individual interviews began the day after the focus group. All of the interviews were conducted in person. The research participants included local professors, students, religious leaders, and professionals. Two participants in the study reported that they had converted their religions. Very few interviews were recorded because the participants did not provide consent, which demonstrated how sensitive this subject was. Neither of the participants who had converted chose to have their interviews recorded. The conversations provided critical knowledge about religious conversions from a local perspective and led to key insights. The research team refined and improved interview questions based upon responses of early research participants, helping to sharpen the focus of the study.

Phase III

During the final days of the fieldwork, the team debriefed to discuss some of the findings using the following indicators. The results will be discussed in the Data and Analysis section.

1. Reported number of religious conversions
2. Reported number of religious conversions related to intermarriage
3. Reported number violent incidents related to religious conversions
4. Number of individuals who have considered changing religions, but reported not carrying through with it
5. Number of individuals who believe they would be disowned by family if they converted to another religion
6. Number of people who believe that religious conversions threatens the region's peace
7. Perception about how easy or difficult it is to change one's religion

The final steps of the project included analysis and development of a report for translation, publication and dissemination. A translated version of this report will be made available to all research participants.

Presentation of Data

Research participants for this study were Christians, Muslims, and Yezidis. Interview questions were tailored specifically for each individual or group. All the research interviews focused on generating data about perceptions of peacefulness, identification of the challenges preventing religious conversion, and the consequences of conversion.

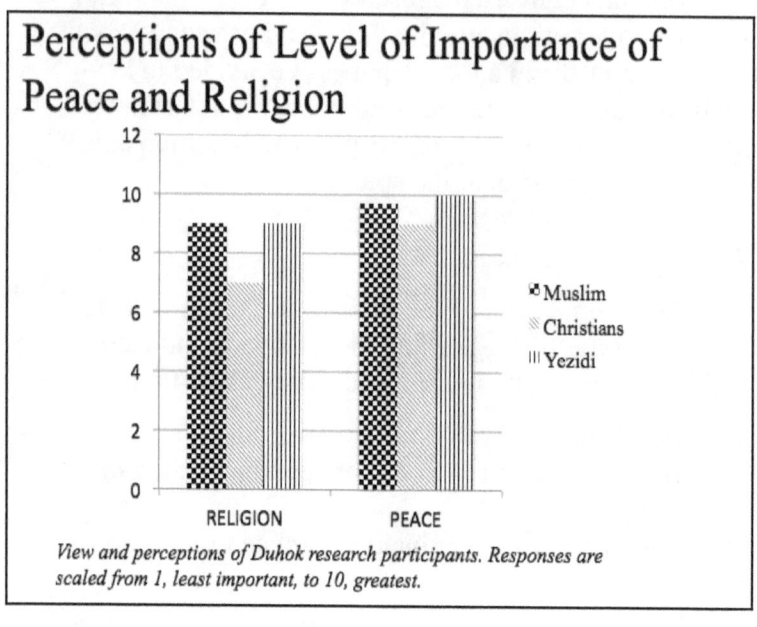

Perceptions of Level of Importance of Peace and Religion

View and perceptions of Duhok research participants. Responses are scaled from 1, least important, to 10, greatest.

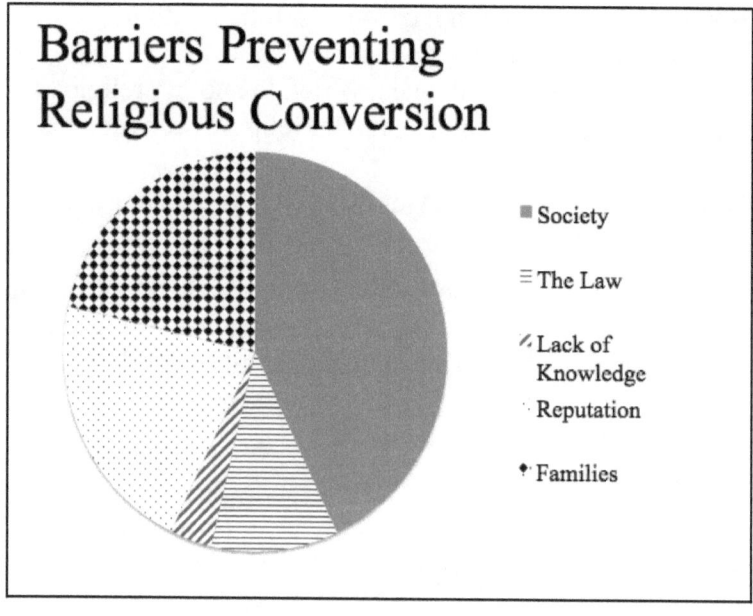

Barriers Preventing Religious Conversion

- Society
- The Law
- Lack of Knowledge
- Reputation
- Families

Perceptions of the Level of Difficulty Converting

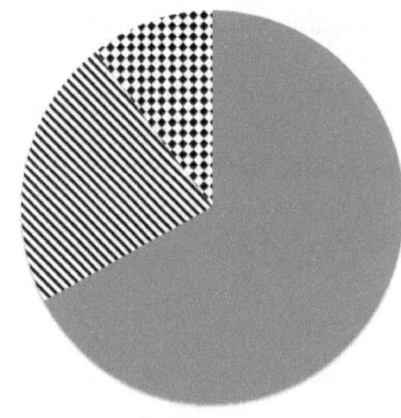

■ Very Difficult

＼ Somewhat Difficult

✦ Not Difficult

Conversion Consequences

INDIVIDUAL	FAMILY	SOCIETY
• Isolated or ostracized • Disowned by family • Damaged reputation with those in old religion • May not be accepted by the new faith • Loss of friends • May have to move to another village or town • Perceived as someone who isn't religious • Perceived as disrespectful to family • May not be able to finish school or stay in profession	• Tarnished reputation in their community • Must reclaim honor – honor killings • May have to leave community or village • Excludes or disowns the individual from the family • May inflict psychological or physical violence	• Changes the community or village ethnic makeup • Causes fissures between members of the community • Challenges social norms and attitudes • Challenges leadership - religious leaders and family • Threatens stability & peace • Violence • Threatens structures put in place by key influencers

Data Analysis

Our team established the seven indicators that we planned to use to draw conclusions, based on primary qualitative and secondary quantitative data, about the relationship between conversion and peacefulness in Duhok. However, much of the supplemental quantitative data we sought was unavailable or inconclusive. The quantitative findings we collected did not contribute to deeper understanding of the relationship between religious conversion and peacefulness in Duhok. Furthermore, collecting qualitative data was also challenging. Below is a summary of the results we gathered, related to the indicators identified above, and the challenges we faced in collecting qualitative data:

- There were no legal reports of religious conversion for any period of time in the Kurdistan Region of Iraq. But we did find two converts who agreed to speak with us anonymously.
- There is intermarriage in Duhok, but the courts do not record religious affiliation on marriage licenses.
- There were no legally recorded cases of violent incidents expressly related to religious conversion.
- Asking participants whether they had given thought to converting was highly sensitive. We did not add the question to the questionnaire, but asked it of participants who demonstrated a willingness to discuss challenging questions. Responses were varied. Some said they never considered conversion. Others believed that it was compulsory for them to remain in the faith into which they were born. Others expressed a feeling that conversion would be worth considering, but did not think that their society would allow them the freedom to convert.
- It is not clear what role the gender, age and social status of those who have converted played in the responses of their families to their conversions. Many participants felt that they would be disowned by their families or isolated if they changed faiths, regardless of age or gender. Of the two converts to whom we spoke, one was male and the other

one was female. The male convert did not lose his family; in fact, his family also converted. The female convert, however, has not spoken with anyone from her immediate family in almost 20 years. Her parents and siblings moved to Bagdad and subsequently to Germany. A larger research sample would be necessary to draw further conclusions about gender and age in relation to religious conversions.

- A majority of the participants believed that religious conversion threatened peace. The primary reason given was that conversion disrupts society.
- All participants, regardless of religious affiliations and social status, concluded that religious conversion was difficult.

Views and perceptions of peace and religion in Kurdistan

All of the research participants said that they considered Duhok a peaceful place. Based on the conversations with research participants, there is a relationship between perceptions of peace in Duhok and the aspiration of those living in the region for an independent state. Anything that threatens social norms and peace may be detrimental to this aspiration. Many participants felt that peace was very important to their region's success and stability.

A shared love of Kurdistan and demonstrations of religious faith were both expressed as essential elements of coexistence, and consequently were fundamental elements of the locally shared definition of peace in the KRI. However, this concept of peace does not take into account the idea that peace should involve the absence of violence of any kind. The participants in this study tended to think only of direct, physical violence, and did not see lack of religious freedom as a form of structural violence that undermines peacefulness.

Another point of view, drawn from research participants' local interpretation of conversion and it's relationship to peace, is that low levels of freedom to change religious groups coincides with high levels of structural violence. Key influencers in families, religious leaders, and parents leverage family power, religious principles, and rhetoric to discourage individuals from conversion. These actions exploit community ties, religious principles, and social status to inflict psychological violence (Galtung 170). Indirect violence is harder to detect because it is rarely reported, physical injuries are not visible, and the outcome is not death, directly.

Barriers that prevent religious conversion

The main deterrents to conversion in the Duhok area are society, family, legal structures, lack of knowledge or education, and the fear of having one's reputation harmed. The social structure in Duhok is designed around small networks of communities where news travels rapidly.

Duhok's society is resistant to change regarding religious conversion. Faith conversion is interpreted as an act of defiance against civility. When civility is disturbed, levels of peacefulness are affected. The underlying issue is that individual choice can cause disorder in society if the actions or decisions of individuals contradict social norms. Consequently, even the thought of conversion clashes with tradition and results in violence, exclusion, or shame.

Families are dominant in Duhok's patriarchal society. It is considered normal for large multi-generational families, including adult children, their spouses, and their children, to occupy one household. This living situation can lead to pressure and suppression of individualism. Reputations are also extremely important. The actions of sons and daughters reflect on parents, aunts and uncles, and other family members. Elders and males influence the way family members behave, although there are many families with strong and vocal female members. Often the principles of faith are used to shape daily lives. Once a person diverges from a family's religion, the principles of that religion can no longer be used as an instrument of coercion. Our research found no evidence of Duhok households composed of family members belonging to different religious groups. Coexistence and acceptance of other religions extended to neighborhoods and communities, but not to individual homes. Therefore, family members to exerted pressure on relatives to remain rooted in the family's religious group.

Moreover, change threatened the power of the familial influencers. According to Johan Galtung, "a person can be influenced not only by punishing him when he does wrong, but also by rewarding him when he does what the influencer considers right. Instead of increasing the constraints on his movement, the constraints may be decreased, instead of increased, and somatic capabilities extended instead of reduced" (Galtung 167-191). In the case of a religious conversion in the KRI, this could mean that drastic action would be taken to redeem the honor of a family and in order to convey a message to other family members that conversion is unacceptable. This is an example of psychological and structural violence as defined by Galtung: "Structural violence is used to threaten people into subordination: if you do not behave, we shall have to reintroduce all the disagreeable structures we had before" (172).

Research participants perceived their respective religious laws as a challenge to religious conversion. According to Sharia law, conversion is not allowed and is punishable by death. The Yezidi faith does not allow conversion and in some cases can carry out honor killings. The Christian bible does not have a specific tenet against conversion, but the denominations in Duhok do not allow conversion or new members. Many people in Duhok depend on their religious leaders to tell them what is allowed in their religions and, in some instances, what the religious law says about conversion. Research participants claimed that there is little knowledge among the general population in Duhok about what the various religious scriptures say about conversions. Residents of the KRI who lack access to educational resources often fall into a role of dependence upon religious leaders and, consequently, become very protective of social customs.

Typical motivations for conversions

The data we collected indicated that the main reasons for conversion were for inter-marriage, the promise of wealth, and improved social status. However, the male convert we interviewed changed his religion from Islam to Christianity because a friend prayed for him and gave him a bible to read. After his conversion, his wife and children changed their religious affiliation as well. He did not lose his job or power of influence. In part, this may have to do with his gender and social and economic status. The other convert interviewed was a female Christian who converted to Islam to marry her husband. As a result, her family disowned her and moved away. At the time of the study, she had not had contact with them for 20 years. She lost life-long friendships. Her in-laws did not embrace her. She reported that they believe that if she was not a faithful Christian, she will never be a faithful Muslim. Her gender and wealth status may have played a role in how she was treated when she converted. Although she was not physically harmed, she endured the effects of structural violence. As Galtung writes, "violence is built into the structure and shows up as unequal power and consequently as unequal life chances" (Galtung 171).

Conclusion

Religious conversion is highly sensitive and controversial in and around Duhok in the Kurdistan Region of Iraq. Our team's attempts to answer core research questions were constructive in some ways and inconclusive in others. This work has generated new information about this matter that can be developed further. The core questions of this research began as follows:

- Why does religious conversion often result in violence?
- Is there a shared definition by the Yezidis, Muslims, and Christians of peace and identity?
- Do local solutions exist that can prevent such violence?
- Are there commonalities between the three religions that can be drawn on as capacities for peace?

Religious conversions seem to exacerbate social tensions in Duhok. Close communities, key family influencers, homogenous households, and collective thought make up some of the social and cultural norms. These norms are perpetually reinforced by religion and perceptions of peace that include the absence of direct physical violence. Even the consideration of religious conversion can lead to structural and psychological violence in Duhok.

Followers of Islam, Christianity, and Yezidism in and around Duhok expressed a shared definition of peace that centered on the lack of direct violence. Based on the interviews the research participants identified as Kurds first and then their respective religious affiliations.

Few research participants interpreted a lack of freedom to convert religious identities as a threat to peacefulness. Further explorations into local peace solutions that can prevent violence, images of peacefulness, and the role of religious conversion in supporting structures of violence are necessary. A deeper study should focus on developing more thorough understandings of how social, legal, and religious structures in Duhok might at once discourage religious conversions and contribute to increased social tensions. This study has raised that question. Further research is needed to answer it.

Works Cited

Akcapar, Sebnem Koser. "Conversion as a Migration Strategy in a Transit Country: Iranian Shiites Becoming Christians in Turkey." *International Migration Review*, Vol. 40.4 (2006): 817-853.

Beehner, Lionel. "Religious Conversion Sharia Law." *Council on Foreign Relations*. 8 June 2007. Web. 20 Feb. 2013

"Four sentenced to death over Du'a Khalil Aswad honor killing." *Ekurd.net*. 30 Mar. 2010. Web. 10 Aug. 2012.

Galtung, Johan. "Violence, Peace, and Peace Research" *Journal of Peace Research*, 6.3 (1969): 167-191.

Gunter, Michael. "The Kurdish Questions in Perspective." *World Affairs*, 166.4 (2004): 197-205.

Human Rights Watch. *Genocide in Iraq The Anfal Campaign against the Kurds*. New York: Human Rights Watch, 1993.

"Iraqi Constitution." *Iraqi Constitution Briefing Committee*. 15 Oct. 2005. Web. 10 Aug. 2012.

Johnson, Toni, and Lauren Vriens. "Islam: Governing Under Sharia (aka shariah, shari'a)." *Council on Foreign Relations*. 9 Jan. 2013. Web. 3 Mar. 2013.

"The status of Christians in the Kurdistan Region in Iraq." *Kurdistan Regional Government UK Representation*. 22 Dec. 2009. Web. 25 Sept. 2012.

Maxwell, Joseph A. *Qualitative Research Design: An Interactive Approach. 3rd Edition*. Los Angeles, CA: Sage Publications, 2013. Print.

"Missing Kurdish Yezidi girl in Iraqi Kurdistan draws intervention of the world's Yezidis." *Edkurd.net*. 2 Feb. 2013. Web. 10 Feb. 2013.

O'Leary, Carole A. "The Kurds of Iraq: Recent History, Future Prospects." *Middle East Review of International Affairs*, 6.4 (2002): n. pag.

Phelps, Sandra Marie. "The Limits of Admittance and Diversity in Iraqi Kurdistan: Femininity and the Body of Du'a Khalil." *Totalitarian Movements and Political Religions*, 11.3–4 (2010): 457–472.

Roy, Sonia. "*The Impact on the Politics of Iraq and Turkey and Their Bilateral Relations Regarding Kurds Post-Saddam Hussein Regime*. Foreign Policy Journal." 22 Apr. 2011. Web. 28 Aug. 2012.

Wong, Edward. "Saddam charged with genocide of Kurds." *New York Times*. 5 Apr. 2006. Web. 28 Aug. 2012.

Ensuring Minority Rights with Reserved Seat Systems in Parliament: Perceptions from the Kurdistan Region and the Disputed Territories of Iraq

By Megan Yasenchak

Research conducted by Megan Yasenchak and Sadiq Hameed

Abstract

Since Iraq's transition to democracy, the federal government has implemented positive accommodation practices to ensure the inclusion and protection of minority rights. One of these measures included the electoral provision in 2009 that guarantees certain ethnic and religious minority groups reserved seats in parliament (eight of 325) at the federal level. Minority groups are not limited to only these seats; they may also elect additional representatives through active political participation with larger political parties. Not all minority groups are represented equally, however, and some groups receive no guaranteed seats. This study discusses perceptions of this system by members of the Christian, Yezidi, and Shabak communities in the Kurdistan Region of Iraq and disputed territories in Iraq as well as by parliamentarians and political experts. The study's focus is to understand whether this measure to guarantee political representation in parliament achieves any minority protection and to what extent it provides safeguards for minority rights. Furthermore, study participants discussed the nature of the electoral system by indicating strengths and weakness in achieving representation.

Introduction

Worldwide, countries have implemented special positive accommodation measures to protect human rights and to encourage minority group participation in elections, whether through special districting, quotas, or guaranteed seat systems. Political inclusion supports multiculturalism and advances human rights, thereby fostering greater social harmony and peacefulness. International frameworks such as the International Covenant on Civil and Political Rights and the Universal Declaration of Human Rights reinforce and embody these critical notions of guaranteeing political and cultural rights for all individuals (United Nations).

As Iraq navigates its political transition from an authoritarian state to an electoral democracy, the country has confronted political challenges in including its diverse ethnic and religious minority groups into its new government. One positive accommodation policy tool Iraq has utilized is the allocated seat system in parliament for specific minority groups, legislated through electoral laws at the federal and regional levels. However, every minority group residing in Iraq does not receive guaranteed seats. Rather, the positions are offered to only specific groups based upon demographic and geographic considerations predetermined by the government (Inter-Parliamentary Union).

With Iraq as a case study, this research project aims to examine the effect of the reserved seat system in Iraq as a safeguard for minority rights Here, this parliamentary positive accommodation policy serves as a reference point to assess political, social and cultural rights in society, The study analyzes minority groups' perceptions of inclusion through social relationships with the government as well as with other ethnic and religious groups. Overall, this paper argues that guaranteeing seats in government is not enough to protect minority rights if other discriminatory structures persist in society. Representation exerts little influence if human rights are not supported consistently and systematically in practice.

Context

The process of reserving seats for ethnic and religious minority groups exists worldwide, including in the countries of the Middle East (Ghai 19). Both the Iraqi central government (since 2009) and the Kurdistan Regional Government (KRG) (since 1992) have allocated reserved seats for minority groups in their respective parliaments. However, these accommodations do not illustrate the full cultural and religious diversity of Iraq. Neither Arabs nor Kurds, as ethnic groups, nor Sunni or Shia Muslims, as sectarian religious groups, receive the reserved seats. It is, rather, the smaller minority groups that have access to these positions in parliament. These smaller minority groups account for just 5 percent of Iraq's entire population. (CIA, "The World Factbook: Iraq"). According to the United States Commission on International Religious Freedom, Iraq's ethnic and religious communities are estimated at: 500,000 Christians, 500,000 Yezidis, 3500-5000 Sabean-Mandaeans, and 2000 Baha'i (USCIRF 98). Ultimately, there are no official demographic records for Iraq since 1987 (Kenyon). Possibilities for a comprehensive census remain uncertain due to group tension regarding the movements of Arabs and Kurds into the disputed territories. Moreover, a census raises political issues regarding regional autonomy statuses and budget allocations contested between the Baghdad central government and the KRG.

Under current electoral law, the Baghdad central government guarantees ethnic and religious minority groups eight seats in parliament (from a total of 325): five seats to Christians, one seat to Yedizis, one seat to Sabean-Mandaeans, and one seat to Shabaks. Of these specified groups, three (Yedizis, Sabean-Mandaeans, and Shabaks) are concentrated in particular geographic regions, receiving only one seat each from their respective governorates; Christians are widely dispersed throughout the country, receiving five seats from five different regions (Interview 1). Likewise, the KRG also instituted a reserved seats system, currently guaranteeing five seats to Christians, five to Turkmens, and one to Armenians – a total of 11 of 110 seats. Nevertheless, in both systems, these seats are only minimum guarantees. Groups may win additional seats through political

candidates and political party support via election results. For
example, six Yezidis are federal parliamentarians in Baghdad
through active participation in political parties during the 2010
election cycle.

Conceptual Framework

This study expands upon several interrelated academic
fields connected to multiculturalism and democracy and
incorporates theories from philosophy, state governance, human
rights and cultural studies. In setting the tone of this study, one
must consider philosopher Charles Taylor's understanding of
identity. "[Identity] is who we are, 'where we're coming from.' As
such it is the background against which our tastes and desires and
opinions and aspirations make sense" (Taylor 33). Taylor's
explanation lays the groundwork for understanding how various
elements shape identity. In the case of ethnic identity, a person's
views may be shaped by his/her membership or experiences in an
ethnic group, drawing from the group's history, perspectives and
narratives.

In accounting for the diversity of identities, theorists have
proposed several elements to foster multiculturalism in society.
Will Kymlicka frames minority rights policies as precautionary
measures against the dominant will of majority groups by
incorporating minority participation into state institutions.
Kymlicka writes, "Majority cultures have typically been equally
contemptuous of the ethnocultural identity and practices of
homeland minorities...[which] have been seen as inferior to the
superior culture of the dominant group" (74). Like Kymlicka,
Sakiko Fukuda-Parr writes that ethnic minorities experience
exclusionary policies due to state practices and warns that
exclusionary policies hamper the overall human development of
the country (41-43).

Nevertheless, theorists remain divided on the impact of
positive accommodation policies for minority groups based solely
upon ethnicity, especially in the political realm. Karen Bird
recognizes the similar challenges shared by gender and ethnicity
groups, but she cautions against "ethnic" minority policies in
political participation due to the inability to classify groups solely

upon ethnic considerations (7-8). Nelson Kasfir presents similar arguments surrounding ethnic classifications. Although Kasfir notes the constraints of ethnic political participation, he acknowledges that ethnic identities incorporate elements of other identities, such as political, class and social thought (374-375).

Although theorists weigh the merits of ethnic considerations in political participation, many states afford some form of positive accommodation policies to their minority groups. Yash Ghai outlines how political participation is a vital human right for minority groups, codified in several United Nations legal frameworks (7). He also identifies positive accommodation policies such as minority representation, power sharing, or autonomy to increase minority presence in government (7-24). Similarly, Andrew Reynolds compiles comprehensive studies of world legislatures. He highlights that several national governments incorporate systems of reserved seats based upon race/ethnicity, language/nation, religion, and geography (19).

Few writings exist that connect these studies to the Middle East or Iraq specifically. Most published explorations on multiculturalism focus on established democracies (Canada, USA, Europe, Australia) and "deeply-divided" democracies where two larger majority groups vie for control (primarily in Africa). Studies focusing directly on the Middle East remain limited. Two such studies including these electoral policies examine Jordan (Fathi) and Lebanon (Laakso). The primary appearances of Iraq's ethnic questions in the literature concern Arab-Kurdish and Sunni-Shia relationships. Adeed Dawisha and Karen Dawisha focus on these major-group divides and caution against majority group ethnic representation in government, arguing that such policies would "cement rather than eradicate ethnic divisions" (36).

Empirical evidence addressing ethnic minority groups' views on their inclusion in political participation remains minimal. One similar study was located, in which Jon Gresham conducted a 2006 survey study on Iraqi perceptions of "out-groups" with Iraqis living in Iraq, Jordan, and the Netherlands (26). Gresham's study analyzes group relationships as some groups returned from exile following the end of Saddam Hussein's regime. The study did not distinguish the smaller ethnic minority groups as separate entities but collectively refers to them as "Other" in relation to "Arab" or "Kurd" groups on the survey forms (Gresham 33).

Therefore, this study contributes to the gaps in the existing literature concerning minority rights and Iraqi studies. Research on the incorporation of ethnic minority groups' rights and democratic participation is timely following Iraq's political transition and the Arab Spring. Furthermore, this study examines minority rights via political participation from the ethnic groups' perspectives, which are also absent from existing studies.

Methodology

Two researchers conducted a series of twenty-three in-person interviews, with thirty-nine respondents, over the course of three weeks in Iraq. The research participants included federal, regional, and local government officials, community leaders, human rights activists, academic experts, and students. None of the minority seat representatives were available for interviews. Conversations were conducted in Kurdish, Arabic, and/or English, with one of the researchers translating the dialogue. Conversations were voice recorded with the participants' consent. All names and identifiers have been removed from this report.

Geographic and security constraints tailored the scope of the research. The research team was based in the Duhok governorate in the KRI, and conducted interviews there, in the disputed territories of neighboring Ninewa governorate, and in Erbil, the capital of the KRI. The team's geographic location influenced the availability of project participants. The primary respondents were self-identified Christians (Chaldean and Assyrian) or Yezidis, as well as one Shabak participant. Additionally, self-identified Kurdish respondents also participated in this study, serving as academic or government experts. There are additional groups living in Iraq, but, due to travel and time constraints, this project was limited in accessing their inclusion. Future research on this subject should attempt to include these groups' perceptions to broaden the scope of the literature.

Similar questions were posed to all research participants, with the goal of assessing the effects of the reserved seat systems. Commonalities and variations in answers were analyzed to account for possible degrees of difference among the respondents. Through qualitative interviews, this study aimed to capture varied narratives on the research topic. Although the study sample cannot be considered representative of Iraq's larger electoral population, it does document narratives and participants' perceptions. These views represent the experiences of these members of society and their groups' relationships to the electoral system, democratic transition, and peacebuilding.

As the overall objective of the study was to assess the protection of political, social, and cultural rights of these minority groups, the reserved seat system served as a reference point by which the participants expressed their views of this positive accommodation practice and its role in fostering peaceful relationships. However, granting seats to protected groups is not enough if there is a missing connection between the parliament and these groups. Therefore, participants were also asked if they perceived any unaddressed needs of their communities that were not met by the government. Additionally, participants also considered their relationships to other groups in the country.

Presentation of Data

Participants, both majority and minority groups members, consistently endorsed the reserved seat system as a means to guarantee minority group participation in Iraq. This measure was seen as necessary to ensure minority access to government representation. Respondents also frequently highlighted the quota for women (25% in the Iraqi federal government and 30% in KRG) with the ethnic and religious groups' seats, linking these two positive accommodation practices together as critical features for addressing political rights for underrepresented communities (Interview 1; Int. 2; Int. 15).

Nevertheless, both participants and political experts saw the reserved seat system as temporary situation, not a guaranteed right. A KRI parliamentarian categorized this accommodation as temporary even though the reserved seats system has been offered in the KRG since 1992, roughly twenty years at the time of this study (Int. 2). A Kurdistan Democratic Party (KDP) representative affirmed that the reserved seat accommodation in the KRI deserves more time as a protective practice (Interview 14). Many participants said that the status of the reserved seat system in both governments is dependent upon the tolerance of diverse minority groups in society. According to the respondents, attitudes of acceptance required additional time. One Christian participant estimated that it would require at least 50 years to alter people's mindsets to vote for someone from another ethnic or religious group (Int. 19).

Participants overwhelmingly agreed that ethnicity and religion play crucial roles in politics and voting practices. Minority group members are free to support any political party of their choice, regardless of affiliation, and larger political parties are encouraged to incorporate candidates regardless of group identities (Int. 14). However, some participants perceived that the larger political parties courted ethnic or religious candidates to draw support away from minority party-supported candidates (Int. 16; Int. 19). Likewise, these participants believed that the larger political parties pressured candidates into supporting the majority's interest rather than working for the needs of their minority group (Int. 16; Int. 19). One Christian participant felt that the minority representatives from regional political parties do not represent the interests of the minority peoples (Int. 19).

An election official highlighted that party support facilitates the nomination process, which requires a security deposit of five million Iraqi dinars ($4167 USD). Financial support from a political party thus allows more people to run for office rather than relying on individual wealth (Int. 21). Relatedly, the advantages and disadvantages of open election lists (selection of any candidate) and closed election lists (selection of party with predetermined list of candidates) were also discussed. A KRI parliamentarian supported closed lists, arguing that it permits flexibility within parties to promote minority candidates on a ranked list (Int. 2). Conversely, an election official supported the open list as a means to advance minority participation, allowing more freedom of choice on the ballots (Int. 21).

Nevertheless, in several conversations participants referenced the 2010 electoral loss of a Yezidi candidate, with good qualifications, who was positioned first on a party's open list but failed to gain enough votes to win a federal seat. This specific example resonated deeply among the Yezidi participants as a case of discrimination through voter preference based upon minority identity and an illustration of why the reserved seats are crucial in protecting minority rights and ensuring political representation (Int. 16; Int. 17; Int. 23).

Participants disagreed on the appropriate number of reserved seats for each minority group. One Christian participant supported the current allocation of five seats in the central government as a fair representation for the Christian community (Int. 8). However, other Christian members believed that the number was insufficient to protect their political and cultural rights (Int. 4; Int. 9; Int. 19). Christian participants also raised concerns that continuous emigration affected their group's ability to ensure stable representation in government (Int. 8; Int. 19).

Yezidi participants criticized the reservation of one seat for their group in the Iraqi parliament. Respondents challenged the distribution of the seats, demanding appropriate increases to reflect the sizes of the minority groups, especially in comparison to the Christian community's allotment (Int. 16; Int. 18). One Yezidi participant noted the success of acquiring six Yezidi federal parliamentarians through party lists in the Ninewa province but expressed the need to guarantee representation of the Yezidi community in case of less favorable elections (Int. 11). A Yezidi human rights activist discussed the same disparities and mentioned a preliminary electoral petition for an increase to four or five seats for the Yezidi minority groups in the 2014 federal elections (Int. 23). Additionally, a former Yezidi parliamentarian also expressed concern over the lack of reserved Yezidi seats in the KRG; in his opinion the Yezidi community deserved at least three guaranteed seats in that parliament (Int. 17).

Participants also noted the representation policy for additional minority groups. A Shabak participant complimented the single reserved seat for his community as a positive feature (Int. 20). However, other participants pointed out that other minority groups received no positive accommodation in elections. Participants acknowledged additional groups – such as the Baha'i, Kaka'i and Abd (Black Iraqis) – who have no guaranteed seats and whose demographic numbers are also critically small in Iraq (Int. 1; Int. 10; Int. 17; Int. 23). Another example is the Turkmen group, which declined seeking reserved seat representation in the federal government. However, one participant believed that three or four seats would be an appropriate number should that group seek guaranteed representation (Int. 1).

Overall, the allocated number of reserved seats (eight of 325) in the Iraqi parliament proved to be too minuscule to advance meaningful political change. If a minority member proposes legislation to benefit its members, additional political support is required from other groups. Participants cited two prominent examples of legislation that promoted minority rights for the Christian and Yezidi communities. One case involved the creation of governmental positions and directorates within the Ministry of Endowment and Religious Affairs (Int. 8; Int. 14; Int. 23). The other piece of legislation was the Personal Affairs law covering marriage and inheritance rights for non-Muslim citizens (Int. 11; Int. 14; Int. 15; Int. 16; Int. 18). This proposed law would provide additional legal protections to religious minority groups. According to the participants, the Personal Affairs law is in its final stages of the review process in the parliament. These two pieces of legislation required multi-party support in order to be established.

When asked if reserved seats created peaceful relations, most respondents mentioned that they make no difference in advancing peaceful intergroup cooperation. One Christian participant referred to the ethnic and religious minority representatives as "axillary members" of parliament (Int. 9). A Shabak participant echoed this sentiment that the representatives possessed no authority in practice (Int. 20). Often, minority groups have been caught between the competing agendas of the majority groups with Arab-Kurdish divisions and Sunni-Shia sectarianism.

Ethnic and religious minority narratives differed based on geographical location. In the Duhok governorate, respondents emphasized the peaceful coexistence of its peoples in its province. In the KRI, where Duhok is located, direct violence is rare. However, participants from the disputed territories responded differently as their narratives on peace are influenced by high levels of direct violence in Ninewa governorate as well as upheavals further south in the country. In Mosul, direct violence is a daily occurrence (Drake).

Geography influences the minority groups' political, social, and cultural needs. In the disputed territories, Christian, Yezidi and Shabak participants all reported that basic needs of utility services and social services of healthcare and education were not provided on a consistent basis (Int. 9; Int. 18; Int. 20; Int. 23). One Christian participant noted the greater reliability of services closer to elections as a means to garner political support (Int. 9). Moreover, the most critical concern for most people was direct violence, as ethnic and religious minorities feared for their future status in Iraq. From the disputed territories, Christian, Yezidi, and Shabak participants demanded greater security protections for their group's survival in the region (Int. 8; Int. 9; Int. 20). These participants viewed direct violence as the primary factor for the accelerating decline of their respective communities (Int. 8; Int. 23). A Christian community leader noted the drastic decline of his community due to emigration – from an estimated 1.5 million to 400,000 nationally and from 500,000 to just 30,000 in Baghdad over the last decade (Int. 8).

Participants attributed the increase in direct violence and victimization of minorities to extremist groups. A federal parliamentarian argued that most direct violence is driven by Iraq's closest neighbors, Turkey, Iran and Syria, reflecting the poor status of coexistence in all of the Middle East (Int. 1). However, other participants noted the rise of "fanatics" inside of the country as the perpetrators of direct violence, thriving on encouraging differences among groups (Int. 12; Int. 23). Additionally, business operations of minority groups are often the targets of direct violence throughout the country (Int. 8). Referencing the December 2011 attacks on liquor stores (in Zakho in the KRI), a Duhok provincial councilmember said that the sale of alcohol by Christians placed these individuals in precarious positions, leaving them vulnerable to attacks and destruction of their personal property (Int.12).

Ethnic and religious minority participants also linked persecution of their groups to the unresolved political status of the disputed territories, resulting in a lack of security provided to them by the state or the KRG. Article 140 of the Iraqi Constitution, which lays out a vaguely-worded roadmap for resolution of territorial disputes, was viewed as affecting the security of minority groups (Int. 9; Int. 18; Int. 20). Participants further held that the failure of the article to be implemented constituted political maneuvering by the central and regional governments and that increased protective measures would be executed once clear authority was established in the disputed territories (Int. 9; Int. 18; Int. 20). One Yezidi community leader shared his insecurity about the disputed administration of these territories (Int. 18). A Christian respondent contested that Ninewa governorate needed greater autonomy to manage its own security affairs and to provide protection for its minorities (Int. 9).

Participants raised issues of land disputes as another form of injustice suffered by minority groups. Within Duhok governorate, Christian participants noted that the Ba'athist regime had seized lands, which, in turn, the KRG inherited and then sold to third parties without legal or financial compensation to the original owners (Int. 19). They noted that members of minority groups traditionally held the lands. An international relief worker confirmed the ongoing status of land disputes throughout Iraq, noting the lack of adjudication measures available for minority groups to resolve communal friction (Int. 22).

Yezidi participants shared persisting concerns related to the Anfal Campaign, which targeted Kurdish populations as well as other ethnic and religious minorities. During the late 1980s, Saddam Hussein's regime attacked the provinces of northern Iraq with military force and chemical weapons, resulting in mass killings, village destructions, and displaced persons. However, minority groups noted a perception of inconsistency in the rebuilding of the destroyed structures among groups, with Christian villages receiving new complexes but Yedizi communities' not receiving resources to meet even their most basic needs, an injustice they said continued even in early 2013 (Int. 16; Int. 18; Int. 23). The same respondents affirmed that they perceived these measures as direct discriminatory practices by both the Iraqi central government and the KRG, favoring Christians over Yezidis (Int. 16; Int. 18; Int. 23). One Yezidi participant contended that Christians received better treatment because of the influence of Western governments, which are more concerned for Christians than other minority groups (Int. 6). A Yezidi human rights activist noted that the Yezidi community is one of the "most ignored groups" in Iraq due to the lack of lobbying efforts worldwide on their behalf (Int. 23).

Participants conceded that the minority groups share common bonds despite the varying levels of political, social and cultural rights offered in Iraq. First, participants acknowledged that ethnic and religious minority groups shared similar histories and experiences. In addition to the reserved seats in parliament, minority participants frequently referenced the Iraqi Constitution as a source of ensuring their human rights. Article 2, Section 2 of the Iraqi Constitution notes the presence of Christians, Yezidis and Sabean-Mandaeans in the country. Notably, the Shabak are not referenced in this document (Int. 20). Nevertheless, for those groups named, the participants appreciated this legal recognition of their religions, with Yezidis acclaiming that it was the first official recognition of their belief as an independent religion (Int. 16; Int. 18).

Christians, however, cautioned against overreliance on the constitution, calling it a work in progress for ensuring rights, equality, and citizenship (Int. 8; Int. 9). Interestingly, Christian participants demanded greater secularism, arguing that religion should be a private matter and that religious categories should be removed from government-issued identification cards (Int. 9). A Christian priest demanded to be treated as a full citizen without always being classified by ethnicity or religion. He believed that eliminating references to identity would foster more unity with "all brothers" in Iraq (Int. 12).

Data Analysis

The interview data produced narratives consistent with patterns expressed by international human rights agencies' reports regarding the protection of minority groups in Iraq (see United States Commission on International Religious Freedom, Minority Rights Group, and Freedom House). Ethnic and religious minority groups remain concerned about their access to political representation and future existence in Iraq. Therefore, adequate and proscriptive protection is required to ensure their rights.

In discussing the positive accommodation policy of the reserved seat system, interesting perspectives existed regarding the origins of this policy and how human rights protections are generated within a state. Political experts expressed an interpretation that the state granted these privileges (a top-down approach), whereas members of the ethnic and religious groups highlighted their action in claiming their human rights and liberties during Iraq's transitional period (a bottom-up approach). Others highlighted the collaborative efforts between the majority and minority groups to implement this policy of accommodation. These perspectives aligned with Kymlicka's caution against the majority will, in which dominant majorities use paternalistic narratives to describe their protection of minority groups.

Likewise, where theorists denounced providing political representation based solely upon ethnic or religious identities, this study uncovered narratives countering that argument. The study's participants felt that their identities provided pathways to political access and recognition suppressed under the Ba'athist regime. In the Iraqi case, minority groups supported retention of the reserved seat system to ensure their inclusion in politics. This support reflects the idea that minorities themselves should determine the utilization of their own group-identity in politics.

This positive accommodation practice remains critical, especially in the cases of smaller minorities, such as the Christians, Yedizis, and Shabaks in Iraq, who have suffered historical and contemporary discrimination by the state and society. Rather than abandon the reserved seat system to ensure ethnically or religiously-blind voting practices, research participants argued that Iraq should retain the reserved system for an indefinite amount of time, at least until society illustrates more tolerance for its multiculturalist reality. In highlighting the inclusion of minority groups into open party lists, larger political parties have attempted a first step towards assisting with the incorporation of marginalized groups in their organizations. However, the wider community of voters must also respond by electing candidates based upon their qualifications, including people from different ethnic or religious groups. Until these practices are a reality, the implementation of reserved seats for these minorities groups must remain in place.

Participants indicated that the reserved seat system had no effect on peacebuilding at the communal level, especially in the disputed territories, where concerns for security, social services and basic needs remained paramount. Participants felt that relying on elections and access to parliamentary seats was ineffective as a method of peacebuilding, mainly because Iraqi minority groups are guaranteed just eight of 325 seats in parliament. When viewing reserved seats for particular groups as a peacebuilding tool, the effectiveness of these measures depended upon the size of the groups. Such representation techniques have more efficiently addressed the needs of countries that are "deeply-divided" democracies (two or more majority groups) as a balancing mechanism, than Iraq, where minority groups receive such a small number of seats in parliament.

Nevertheless, the reserved seat system has fostered greater coordination among the ethnic and religious minority groups. Although some regional divides exist, group identity and membership has overshadowed some geographical concerns. Minority group participants, Christian, Yezidi, and Shabak alike, expressed concern for their respective group members regardless of location in Iraq. The participants also recognized numerous cross-minority group challenges that all of their members faced together, whether politically, socially, or culturally.

In Iraq's transition to democracy, the positive accommodation practice of reserving seats for minority groups attempts to address the needs of its ethnically and religiously diverse population. However, the number of seats reserved remains too small to facilitate the significant changes required to adequately assist these minority communities. First and foremost, channels of communication must remain open between these parliamentarians and their constituents to ensure political, social, and cultural rights. Furthermore, the reserved seats must be viewed as an affirmative action policy to include ethnic and religious minority members in government and to protect their rights to the fullest extent, rather than a peacebuilding measure for these groups.

The practice of reserving seats for Iraq's minority groups in parliament illustrates the multi-faceted landscapes of political, social and cultural challenges for these groups in the country. As minorities continue to experience declining numbers in their population, greater emphasis must be placed on the protection of their minority rights. The campaign to ensure ethnic and religious minority groups' existence cannot be only advanced by their representatives but must also be championed by the whole of parliament and at all levels of society. In Iraq, these groups' perceptions of political and social inclusion are not simply their views, but are also an intertwined narrative of how Iraq has transitioned as an independent, democratic nation.

Works Cited

Bird, Karen. "The Political Representation of Women and Ethnic Minorities in Established Democracies: A Framework for Comparative Research." Presented at the Academy of Migration Studies in Denmark (AMID), Aalborg University11 Nov. 2003. Web. 8 Aug. 2012.

Central Intelligence Agency. "The World Factbook: Iraq." Web. 8 Aug. 2012.

Dawisha, Adeed and Karen Dawisha. "How to build a Democratic Iraq." *Foreign Affairs*, 82:3 (May/June 2003): 36-53. Web. 8 Aug. 2012.

Drake, John. "Mapping Violence in Iraq." *Iraq-Business News*. 11 Nov. 2011. Web. 16 May 2013.

Fathi, Schirin. "Jordanian Survival Strategy: The Election Law as a 'Safety Valve.'" *Middle Eastern Studies*, 41:6 (Nov. 2005): 889-898. Web. 16 May 2013.

Freedom House. "Freedom in the World 2012: Iraq." Web. 16 May 2013.

Fukuda-Parr, Sakiko. "Cultural Freedom & Human Development Today." *Daedalus*, 133:3 (Summer 2004): 37-45. Web. 16 Aug. 2012.

Ghai, Yash. *Public Participation and Minorities*. Minority Rights Group. London: Minority Rights Group (2001). Print.

Gresham, Jon. "Iraqi Perceptions of 'Out-Groups': Effects of Ethnicity, Religion, and Location." *Digest of Middle East Studies*, 15:2 (Fall 2006): 26-40. Web. 16 Aug. 2012.

Inter-Parliamentary Union. "Council of Representatives of Iraq: Electoral System." Web. 8 Aug. 2012.

Interviews 1-23. Confidential. Personal Archive. Jan. 2013. Available upon request.

Kasfir, Nelson. "Explaining Ethnic Political Participation." *World Politics*, 31:3 (1979): 365-388. Web. 8 Aug. 2012.

Kenyon, Peter. "In Iraq, Counting Heads is a Political Headache." *National Public Radio*. 20 Oct. 2010. Web. 16 May 2013.

Kymlicka, Will. "Do We Need Minority Rights." *Constellations*, 4:1 (1997): 72-87. Web. 8 Aug. 2012.

Laakso, Liisa. "Ethnicity in World-System Perspective: The Case of Lebanon." *Current Research on Peace and Violence*, 12:4 (1989): 176-190. Web. 16 May 2013.

Minority Rights Group. "Iraq's Minorities: Participation in Public Life." 2011.Web. 21 Feb. 2013.

Reynolds, Andrew. *Electoral Systems and the Protection and Participation of Minorities*. London: Minority Rights Group (2006). Print.

Taylor, Charles. "The Politics of Recognition." *Multiculturalism: Examining the Politics of Recognition*. Ed. Amy Gutman. Princeton: Princeton University Press (1994): 25-73. Web. 8 Aug. 2012.

United Nations. "The International Covenant on Civil and Political Rights." *United Nations Treaty Series*, Vol. 999: 171. Web. 16 May 2012.

United Nations. "The Universal Declaration of Human Rights." Web. 16 May 2012.

United Nations Global Issues. "Democracy and Human Rights." Web. 16 Aug. 2012.

United States Commission on International Religious Freedom. "Annual Report 2012." 2013. Web. 16 May 2012.

Perceptions and Realities of Women's Rights in the Kurdistan Region of Iraq: A Case Study of Akre Community

By Katarzyna Szutkowski

Abstract

Despite the significant progress in the Kurdistan Region of Iraq toward embracing women in reconstruction efforts, the promotion of women's involvement in peace and security initiatives continues to be overlooked. Numerous reports of political exclusion, limitations in power sharing, and the denial of women's rights and their economic development continue to surface. The empowerment and engagement of women in all sectors and at all levels is necessary for the future peace of the Kurdish Region of Iraq. Promotion of a gender quota for women's representation in the Kurdish Regional Government Parliament has proven to be insufficient for strengthening women's capacity and promoting their rights. This study is a local assessment, including of a rural community area, and analysis of various fundamental concepts: gender, education, political participation, family structure, patriarchy, and violence. It also represents women's own views and opinions on what shapes and effects their participation within communities, society's perception of them and women's perceptions of themselves; it represents women's own reflections and their own experiences.

Introduction

In the past decade, the social and political climate in the autonomous Kurdish region of Northern Iraq has undergone a significant transformation. For Kurds, progress towards democracy, stability, and peace continues to be at the forefront of the nationalistic development agenda, modestly integrating the country's female population. The Constitution and its recommendations resulted in an increased number of women represented in Kurdish Parliament and the amendment of the Family and punitive codes. Women are allowed to hold positions in the judicial system and are now present in the media and at universities. In contrast with still-fragile Iraq, these visible changes suggest that the Kurdistan Region of Iraq (KRI) is a success story for Iraq and an example for the region. It also implies that Kurdish women enjoy more independence and freedom than neighboring Iraqi women.

In this study, I dispute the reality of the reported progress in the KRI, where a highly male-dominated society continues to subject and exploit women, decreasing their input into the development of the KRI. Low indicators in women's higher education and political participation are not the attributes of a progressive society. Despite a fair number of female members of parliament (MPs), Ms. Asos Najib Abdullah is the only woman holding a ministerial position in the Sixth Cabinet of the Kurdish Regional Government (KRG). The previous KRG Cabinet had three female ministers, in contrast with the sole female minister in the present cabinet. This decline suggests an unbalanced distribution of resources (e.g. education, workforce participation), benefits, and opportunities to women, while demonstrating a lack of women's perspectives on socio-economic, cultural, and political matters.

Traditional attitudes towards women have not changed much. According to the Iraqi Knowledge Network 2011, gender-based discrimination towards women in education and employment continues to affect the region's social and economic development. In Akre, all the women and men I interviewed agreed that women are still facing many obstacles in society. In this paper I review the family pressures, economic dependence, and lack of freedom that women face and the trends of violence against women in the KRI. Primary data from this study as well as secondary sources and quantitative indicators demonstrate that addressing women's status in the KRI, in addition to regional economic development and a stable political environment, is imperative.

Conceptual Framework and Methodology

To properly assess the social position of Kurdish women in Iraq, their activities, their changing status vis-à-vis men, and their potential leadership capacities in communities, I used a framework originally created by sociologist Janet Giele and further developed by Valentine M. Moghadam in her study on social change and its impact on and involvement of women in the Middle East, North Arica and Afghanistan. For the purpose of this paper, I analyzed, in detail, three out of six proposed dimensions:[1]

1. Political expression: What rights do women possess, formally and otherwise? How are they involved in the political process?
2. Education: What access do women have and how much can they attain?
3. Family and violence within the family: What is the status of women? Do family laws empower or disempower women?

To fully understand what shapes and affects women's participation within communities, I investigated society's perception of women and women's perceptions of themselves, their own image, and their own experiences. The research was divided into two phases: research design and preparatory desk research in New York for five months in 2012 and a three-week field research in January of 2013 in the KRI. The on-the-ground research was carried out in three different areas of the KRI: Duhok, Akre, and Erbil. This paper focuses on the findings from Akre.

While abroad, I conducted twelve semi-structured interviews among students, professionals, men, and women

---

[1] The full six are political expression, work and mobility, family, education, health and sexual control, and cultural expression.

activists and hosted one focus group. I talked to Members of the
Kurdish Parliament from the main Kurdish political party of
Massoud Barzani, the Kurdish Democratic Party (KDP), in Erbil[2]
and in Akre. There were two categories of interviews:

- Formal interviews with government officials,[3] members of
  educational institutions, and members of non-governmental
  organizations (NGOs) with governmental and non-
  governmental affiliations.[4]
- Less formal interviews with average women and men, who
  were more relaxed, yet incredibly emotionally and
  intellectually charged.[5]

The focus group discussion was comprised of only female
participants and took place at the Women's Union, an organization
supported by the KDP. All the interviews were recorded and
translated with the help of local translators.

I also reviewed and compiled secondary sources. The fact
that Kurdish women's history, culture, politics, life, and sexuality
have been long ignored, as Shahrzad Mojab so eloquently explains
in her books, did pose some difficulties in obtaining and studying
the context. However, visiting the country allowed me to access
local resources. The access to the Women's Union in Akre and the
statistics provided by the Technical Institute of Akre allowed me to
view numerical data otherwise unavailable in the United States.
The majority of the sources reviewed were available in English;
some, if in Kurdish, were translated by the local translators.[6]

---

[2] Erbil is called Hawler in Kurdish.
[3] These interviews were conducted in the cities of Akre and Erbil. The Member
of the 9th District of KDP was interviewed in Akre, and two female Members of
Parliament were interviewed in Erbil.
[4] In Kurdistan the majority of NGOs are affiliated with the government or a
political party, including sponsorship and financial support.
[5] Some of these discussions took place in cars, stores, and on the grounds of the
Technical Institute of Akre. All Kurdish women that I had a chance to interview
were extremely accepting, loving, and kind. I am forever grateful and extremely
humbled for this experience.
[6] The local translator was hired and available while I was in Kurdistan. She also
worked with me for the duration of this project, while I was in United States.

Perception versus Reality

Women's Political Participation

In the past decade some progress has been made in the political participation of Middle Eastern women. Gender norms have been improved to some extent (Moghadam 441-449). However, the level of women's political participation, their educational attainment, and social equality remain trifling.

The most conventional concept of participation in political science includes a wide-range of activities and time devoted by a particular member in an organization or clubs. Such activities, called "political participation," intend to influence local or national policies, government, or "political staff" (Whiteley 1). The literature separates political participation into two categories – high-intensity and low-intensity participation. Although both types of political participation aim at influencing policies, high-intensity participation has elevated costs in time and effort and is the least accessible. While low-intensity participation, which involves voting, signing petitions, supporting a party, volunteering, or donating time and money, may seem to carry less weight, its collective influence must not be underestimated (Martineau 1). These activities are essential in supporting institutions and are responsible for party and organization success. "Political parties are the most important non-state institutions in democratic politics," but they are only strong because "partisanship [is] a strong force in electoral politics" (Martineau 2).

Adopted in 1948, the Universal Declaration of Human Rights guarantees "fundamental freedoms without distinction of any kind, such as race, colour, sex, language, religion, political or other opinion, national or social origin, property, birth or other status" (Article 2). But despite the declaration, women continue to experience widespread discrimination and exclusion from participation in and contribution to society. Women's participation in public life has improved globally with the implementation of the Convention to Eliminate of All Forms of Discrimination Against Women (CEDAW), adopted by the United Nations (UN) General Assembly in 1979, the adaptation of the Beijing Platform for Action (PFA) in 1995, and UN Security Council Resolution 1325 on Women, Peace and Security, approved in 2000. Despite a slight increase in women in legislative positions – from 10.1 percent in 2010 to 11.3 percent in 2012 – women in Arab States are still the least represented in Parliaments worldwide at an average of 19.7 percent.

Table 1. Women's Representation in Parliaments and Ministerial Positions 2010-2012

	Lower/Single House 2010	**Lower/Single House 2012**
World Average	19.0%	19.7%
Nordic countries	42.1%	42.0%
Americas	22.1%	22.6%
Europe OSCE[a]	19.9%	20.8%
Sub-Saharan Africa	18.4%	20.4%
Asia	18.7%	18.3%
Pacific	13.2%	12.4%
Arab States	10.1%	11.3%

In spite of some progress, the position of women in the KRI is far from a success story. The high rates of female illiteracy (24% to 33% for women age 12 and higher), high unemployment among women (only 12.3% of females employed for wages), insufficient access to health facilities, and lack of mental health education and support are alarming (CSO). The level of female representation, interest in, and access to leadership positions at the local or regional levels is also unsatisfactory. Sozan Arif, Director and Chair of the Women's Empowerment Organization located in Erbil, acknowledged in a phone interview in 2013 that most improvements in the KRI are purely decorative.[7] There are many

---

[7] Women Empowerment Organization is an independent organization established in June 2004; Erbil, Iraq. For more information see http://www.weoiraq.org/

debates on women's rights, but in reality there is neither a solid plan nor an interest in challenging the existing status quo.

> This is a problem; there is no real participation of women in Kurdistan (KRI). There are many reasons: social, unsupportive mentality of the community, legislations, discrimination, lack of development, etc. The most important is that there is no preparation for women to become active. Women lack confidence and knowledge of their rights and responsibilities.

There is also a lack of confidence in women's political decision capabilities among local men. During my interview in Akre, when I asked a young male office worker if he thinks women are making decisions along with men about the future of the KRI, he replied "[...] women are not capable to make right decision about the country, not here in Kurdistan, [it] is impossible in Kurdistan. Whatever the intelligence woman has, she is a woman after all and could not be successful."

Aveen Omar Ahmad, a member of the Kurdish Parliament, believes that widely acceptable and perpetuated patriarchal practices in Kurdish society are responsible for women's under-representation.

> Our society is directly related to our traditions and customs. This strongly affects women's participation in [the] political sphere. Also, men who are working in political positions, they are part of the society; men are growing up with these traditions. [We] have a label that women should participate, but reality is different.

For women who enter politics, the environment within and outside of political parties seems to be unsupportive and critical. According to Ahmad (MP), the current socio-political atmosphere requires women leaders to demonstrate, loudly and clearly, their qualifications and skills to do the job. She argued that women have to work extra hard to ensure their position, "not like men." She said:

> [A woman] needs double efforts to persuade, to be listened and to have her point taken under consideration. Even now when women are competing for the political

positions, for man is easier to get the vote. … [W]hen it comes to decision-making process you will see that women do their absolute best to gather data and collect information, so that the decision-making can be done in a proper way. In our society women are viewed as only for taking care of children, family, and [so] it is strange for men to see strong women with powerful opinions that people can follow. This is difficult for [men] to see.

Table 2. Women's Appointments and Representation through 1 January 2012, Selected Arab States

| Country | Lower/Single House | | | | Ministers | | | |
	Rank	Total Seats	No. of Women	% Women	Rank	Total	No. of Women	% Women
Iraq	38	325	82	25.2	91	26	1	3.8
KRI (Kurdistan Region of Iraq)[b]	--	111	43	38.7	--	19	1	5.2
Kuwait	122	65	5	7.7	86	16	1	6.3
Lebanon	135	128	4	3.1	96	29	0	0
Libya	No Parliament as of January 2012				78	24	2	8.3
Syria	97	250	31	12.4	71	30	3	10
United Arab Emirates (UAE)	75	40	7	17.5	46	22	4	18.2
Yemen	142	301	1	0.3	79	37	3	8.1
Jordan	106	120	13	10.8	84	30	2	6.7
Saudi Arabia	143	150	0	0	96	26	0	0

Source: Compiled from statistics available from the Inter-Parliamentary Union (IPU) web site, 'Women in Politics: Situation on 1 January 2012", www.ipu.org. For the KRG, information was compiled from the KRG Government (KRG) website www.krg.org and based on the information obtained from the interview at the Parliament.

a. Europe OSCE Nordic countries not included
b. KRG region is not recognized as an autonomous state, and as such not in the ranking system.

To tackle under-representation, the implementation of an electoral gender quota has been introduced in over 100 countries worldwide (Ballington; Karam 142; Takagi et al). In the KRI, the fulfillment of the quota provision was introduced to emphasize women's role in political life. Both the law establishing Iraq's Independent High Electoral Commission (IHEC) and the draft Constitution of the KRG recommended that women comprise at least 30 percent of political party lists and in the Iraqi Kurdish Parliament (Iraq IHEC, National Assembly of Iraqi Kurdistan of Iraq-Iraq). As a result, 43 out of 111 members of the Kurdish Parliament are female, making up over 38 percent of the total elected members of the legislative body (Ahmad).

The interviews conducted among students and faculty members at the Technical Institute of Akre and in the discussion group indicated that for the majority of women, especially young women 18 to 35 years old, having a gender quota is very important; out of 28 women, 24 (85%) indicated that the parliamentary quota system is of high importance. Feiruz Taha Akrawi, an Active Member of the 9th Branch of the Kurdish Democratic Party (KDP) in Akre, recommended an increase of female representation at the national level to empower women at the regional level to get more involved and active in their own communities.

Quota implementation, however, does not appear to be sufficient to change the masculine model of politics in the KRI. Since 1991, when the KRG opened up space for women in key positions, not much improvement has been achieved in terms of political equalities and women's empowerment. Asos Najib Abdullah, Minister of Labour and Social Affairs, is the only woman out of the 19 ministers of the Sixth Cabinet of the Kurdish Regional Government (KRG). In contrast, the previous KRG Cabinet had three women in ministerial positions.

"The situation is frustrating," said Lanja Abdulla, Director of the Warvin Foundation located in Erbil, an independent organization for women's issues. She believes the main reason for the meager support of female leaders is not a lack of qualifications, but their disengagement with the society and lack of attention to the critical needs of Kurdish women. One problem, according to

Abdulla, is the parties' electoral process. Abdulla agrees that having a set number of women represented at the decision-making level is a positive sign, but she notes that "most of those who are the candidates of their political parties they represent themselves not the people, sometimes they have to do what they are told, instead of what they feel or what should do." This sentiment resonated among many interviewed women, who pointed out a lack of commitment by female leaders, lack of willingness to build relationships with the female population, and insufficient attention by female political leaders to improve women's position in society.

The struggle of independent women's and human rights organizations was also evident. In the KRI, the general perception of politics as *men's business* remains, with only 68 percent of women believing that women are capable of participating in political elections as candidates. While women's engagement in political affairs is low, the perception on voting is more satisfactory: 95.1 percent believe women should vote, and among women 15 to 54 years of age, 78 percent participated in 2010 elections (CSO). Out of 28 women I interviewed in Akre, 23 (82%) indicated they are registered to vote and had voted at least twice previously. Twenty-three also felt that taking part in elections is very important for women. Akrawi, a KDP leader said:

> I am now very optimistic that the eagerness that we
> found in women is higher than in men in voting terms;
> especially, if it belongs to casual elections, addressing
> Kurdistan's affairs and [the] future. [...] when they see
> that there is something so important such as future of the
> Kurdistan they will participate.

Low-intensity participation among women within communities however, has not improved much. Despite the increased interest in politics among the female population since 2005, only 7.9 percent of women are active in social clubs, unions, or women's associations (CSO). Women in rural areas seem to be in an even worse position. Women I interviewed at the Women's Union in Akre indicated that women's participation is not encouraged by existing political, male population and religious leaders, there is a need for support for women wanting to contribute to the community, and agreed that there were no prospects for decision-making positions in the community. Women did not feel that engaging women at the local level was a priority for and or that there was an interest in addressing the lack of opportunities for women among the current political leaders in the community.

Akrawi underlined the lack of attention given to the rural areas: "here, Akre is [a] more tribal area and it needs more help, more support, more courses to educate [women], we need more attention to make women active and successful." She indicated that women's turnout in meetings and community discussions is high in the inner city of Akre, but "participation rates drop drastically the further one moves outside of the city." She felt that participation is low because of a lack of professional education for women and patriarchal social structures that do not encourage women to be socially active in public.

Some activities are available to women in Akre – mainly workshops on sewing and nursing. According to Mustafa Saleen, director of the Aynda Organization for Society Awareness in Akre, only a few of the of 300 seminars given within the community focused on the "Role of Youth in the Political Process;" the rest concentrated on violence against women. No seminars were given on leadership, governance, the role of women in peacebuilding, reconstruction, strengthening democracy, or empowerment.

Education

Changes to the education system were introduced to Iraq and its northern region at the beginning of 1996, when UNESCO constructed hundreds of schools and distributed textbooks and educational materials (UNESCO). Since then, some progress in terms of primary school enrollment has been made in Iraq and the KRI. The net enrollment in primary schools for girls in the overall country is 87.4 percent, versus 77 percent in rural areas (MISC). The ratio drops significantly, however, in net enrolment in secondary schools to slightly over 44 percent for females (and 52.5 percent for males).

Statistics provided by the Technical Institute of Akre (a public institution that provides two year degrees), suggested a positive shift in female participation and graduation from the college, but the ratio of female to male students was still low. In Table 3 below, the number of female students accepted has increased in the last decade from 18 in 2000 to 230 in 2011. During the same period, the acceptance of male students grew from 10 to almost 300, with a peak of more than 500 accepted in 2010. The overall percentage of male student attendance and graduation rate from the Institute in the last ten years is nearly twofold that of the female students: 64 percent of male versus 36 percent female graduated. There is an apparent difference in the graduation rate of female students versus their male counterparts, which can be seen in the data table below. Compared to the overall acceptance level for each academic year, the total percentage of female students graduating, when compared to the number of both males and females accepted, is higher than that of male students.

Data provided by University of Duhok, a four year institution, presented in Table 4, suggests a similar trend in the graduation rate of female students versus their male counterparts. Generally, the percentage of female students graduating from the University, compared to the total number of female and male students accepted, is higher than that of male students.

Table 3. Male vs. Female Acceptance and Graduation Rates, Technical Institute of Akre

Years	Accepted		Graduated	
	Female	Male	Female	Male
2000-2001	18	10	0	0
2001-2002	32	37	16	6
2002-2003	27	59	28	32
2003-2004	38	93	19	52
2004-2005	13	48	29	43
2005-2006	18	84	11	29
2006-2007	46	141	17	65
2007-2008	95	199	29	72
2008-2009	176	392	65	110
2009-2010	271	507	148	260
2010-2011	230	298	210	343
Total %	**34.0%**	**65.9%**	**36.1%**	**63.8%**

Source: Compiled from statistics provided by the Office of Planning, Technical Institute of Akre, 2013.

Table 4. Male vs. Female Students Acceptance and Graduation Rates, University of Duhok

Years	Accepted		Graduated	
	Female	Male	Female	Male
2000-2001	N/A	N/A	146	206
2001-2002	N/A	N/A	209	227
2002-2003	1249	1652	199	275
2003-2004	1650	2021	228	331
2004-2005	1999	2450	309	364
2005-2006	2811	3291	365	375
2006-2007	3217	3839	547	609
2007-2008	3993	4996	591	703
2008-2009	4281	5509	877	1083
2009-2010	5000	5880	839	880
2010-2011	N/A	N/A	909	910
Total %	44.94%	55.0%	46.6%	53.3%

Source: Compiled from statistics provided by Office of International Relations at University of Duhok 2013. Statistics were not available for the academic year 2000-2002 and 2010-2011.

Cumulatively across the last ten years, female student participation is higher in the urban setting (University of Duhok) versus the rural area (Technical Institute of Akre). Over the past ten years female to male attendance ratios were 1:1.2 for the University of Duhok and 1:1.9 for the Technical Institute of Acre – a nearly equal female-to-male participation ratio in the urban area but only one female for every two male students in the rural area.

Despite of the improvements, the education system in the KRI remained challenging. The Minister for Higher Education, Dlawer Abdul Aziz Ala'Aldeen, aware of the government's disregard for progress and lack of a long-term plan to revive the level of higher education in the KRI, planned to introduce a series of improvements at both the master's and bachelor's levels. The planned changes were promising: expanded courses to other centers so that women who cannot travel can continue their education, faculty selection based on expertise and specialty, improved quality-assurance of teaching and conducted research and finally, improved curricula (Ministry of Higher Education and Scientific Research).

The illiteracy rate among women in the KRI was high at 32 percent – significantly higher than the rest of the Iraqi governorates at 19.6 percent (CSO). The female illiteracy rate has also been higher in rural areas (36.5 percent) than in urban areas (15.9 percent). As girls' attendance at the primary level in the KRI remains satisfactory, the significant dropout appears at the secondary level (in rural areas) and higher education. Over 70 percent of interviewed women in Akre indicated that male-controlled traditions and customs have negatively affected women's access to education. During the discussion with women at the Women's Union in Akre, one woman said:

> The biggest difference [in rural areas] is that when a girl finishes her 6th class/grade she would be stopped by her family to go to school. Tradition plays a big role. Our society is still backward, men own everything here and women are under the gun.

Also, the community state of mind seemed to remain the same. During the interview with the Head of Office of Planning at the Technical Institute of Akre, he summarized: "I do not think girls have an opportunity to go to the political side here, girls get the benefit from the Institute for the society; they are work as nurses at the local hospital."

In the KRI, women continue to have limited access to political power and economic independence. They also suffer from a general lack of support for women's education that has barred them from equal opportunities and self-realization. The deeply rooted traditional family values also continued to dominate, leaving decisions to be made by men in their lives.

Social Structure

Historically, Kurdish society has been highly male-dominated. Household relations reflected specific gender arrangements where Kurdish women, *kabanî*, remained subordinate to men, *malxî* (Al-Khayyat 17). The patriarchal arrangement affected women's status and formed gender inequalities. It reinforced prejudicial behavior towards women and pressured individuals to conform to specific behavioral patterns. Women's subordination to men is reflected in customary Kurdish practices: polygamy,[8] arranged marriages (often without female consent), or offers of marriage, *shirbayee*, in exchange for money or to settle tribal conflicts (Hardi 3). One interview participant in Akre said:

> Men don't understand what the rights of other humans are, they understand if they ask their women, they lost control over them. This is not right. [I]n case of marriage there is an exchange of women as well. To solve their ravages cases they offer a girl as an exchange for another family to solve the problem. [...] They sell women and girls for money.

A woman I interviewed in Akre disclosed that the gap between men and women in the family also affects daughter-father relationships. She explained,

> I think the main reason behind killing women is family itself, the members and the male figure, father, brother, even uncle. They don't have good relationships with daughters; fathers with his daughter, or brother with his sister. [...] here is a great gap between the two: male and female in the family. So, [t]hey support a boy to continue his study to do everything, but not a girl, she cannot even choose a husband for herself.

The interviewed women also reported that girls get into trouble when they look for the love, acceptance, and admiration they have not received at home. While publicly speaking with male peers is not acceptable in Kurdish tradition,[9] young people form relationships over the Internet and use their mobile phones to stay connected. For some female teenagers, such activities are met with anger, violence, or even death from their family members.

In the KRI, girls are exposed to the ideology of *sharma* and *aiba,* honor and shame. The concept of *sharma* is linked to sexual

---

[8] Although restricted by the KRG, polygamy is still a practiced custom.
[9] Unless at schools, which was very refreshing to observe while I had a chance to spend few days at the Institute of Akre's cafeteria talking to students and faculty members.

conduct of women; once a woman breaks the rules, the whole family is humiliated. If a woman's so-called misconduct becomes public, her reputation and the family's reputation become irreparable, reflecting especially badly on the male figure. A female student in Akre explained that the social control of women plays out through gossip: "People are talking, compare, tell on others, and question your family, [there is] too much talking." Gossip "operates as one of the strongest forms of social control, particularly in policing women" (Al-Khayyat 23). Girls live in constant fear of disobeying social norms and of accusations of misconduct. A picture taken at the Women's Union in Akre summarizes the grave consequences of gossip.

"Don't let people's chatter and rumors be your decider for finishing [hurting or killing] our women and girls, raise up.

NO for abuse"

In the KRI, violence toward women is common. Until 2002, the Penal Code contained an "honourable motives" clause in cases of violence against women. And although the clause was repealed, not much changed for women in the region. Out of the 30 women interviewed, 29 reported that violence against women is frequent and generally accepted by the community. Twenty-six women reported experiencing violence or knowing someone who had killed a female relative or had been killed by a family member(s). Interview participants said that authorities do not investigate these crimes properly and do not prosecute those who supported the killer; everyone acts as if the crime did not happen. If the girl survives, the act is disguised under the attempt of suicide. The killer(s) is sheltered by the tribe, family and surrounding community.[10]

During the focus group discussion, I asked if there is any support from the community leaders or a place where a woman can seek shelter if she feels threatened. One woman explained that they had asked for such support many times, but nothing had been provided.

Abdulla (of the Warvin Foundation), who conducted several surveys on sexual assault, violence against women, and honor killings in KRI, described her irritation with the current situation and the ignorance of leaders who declare their commitment to improve women's status and their position. She said:

> Until now, we kill a woman in this society because she loves a guy! There is no power; absolutely there is no power that women can use. Political party, government, religion, and society they are all against women. Even when political parties and government talk about women's issues is like a joke for them instead of just takes care of this. Until now, they not have realized the importance, you know, of the sensitivity of these issues.

In addition to the patriarchal system, religion is a contributing factor to the subjugation of women in Kurdish society. For many Muslim men and women who I interviewed, the role of Islam and Imams remains very powerful. The majority felt the religion itself is not an obstacle for women's equality and source of women's subordination and submissiveness, but rather how the religion is interpreted. Other women, however, disagreed. One woman during the interview in Akre reported that an Imam had

---

[10] Over the course of several days during my visit to Akre, three different women mentioned a recent murder that took place in the area. A young girl was allegedly killed for spending too much time at her neighbor's house. All three women complained that there was not enough time spent on the investigation and the family protected those who committed the crime. These reports were consistent with the 2009 Amnesty International Report *Trapped by Violence, Women in Iraq*, which states that "many men who commit violent crimes against women are never brought to justice because the authorities are unwilling to carry out proper investigations and punish the perpetrators" (4).

been "distributing CD and cassettes, not from the KRI maybe from Saudi Arabia that encouraging people to do violence against women, [...] they urge people to kill women when they do not obey their [husbands]."

Many women were also disappointed by the absence of Imams' stand on conversations on women's rights in the KRI. Religious leaders play a critical role in leading toward positive transformation and social equality. Participants suggested that both the Government and religious leaders should work together if they are committed to effectively combatting the ongoing discrimination and violence towards women.

In the meantime, KRI Prime Minister Nechirvan Barzani on December 2012 announced a 16-day Campaign on Violence Against Women, calling it "a terrible expression of inequality and injustice" (KRG). He stated during the inauguration that this campaign is the government's fight for women's rights, elimination of discrimination, inequalities and aggression against women.

Conclusion

The progress toward democratization and modernization of the Kurdistan Region of Iraq remains critical. The slow pace of women's empowerment and their exclusion in decision-making roles continues to raise concern for the region. As the country continues to work toward its transformation, a lack of focus on women's empowerment continues to raise concern. As the need for empowerment and engagement of women in all sectors and at all levels is necessary for the future peace in the region, the promotion of the Parliamentary quotas for women proved to be insufficient for strengthening women's capacity and promotion of their rights. Furthermore, lack of political knowledge, rights and responsibilities discourage many women, especially those of younger generations, from playing an active role within the community. Active guidance and local leadership support may prove to be constructive tools to increase future participation and spark the interest for future involvement. Furthermore, poor performance assessments of the members of parliament suggest a lack of tangible and solid improvements and the need for engagement with the population.

Increased peacefulness in the Kurdish Region of Iraq cannot be contingent only on regional economic development, increased capacity for self-governance, and a stable political environment. Strategic plans for rebuilding, mobilizing the population, and protecting and strengthening social capacity must mobilize the entire "country's human resources" (Moghadam 337) including its women, all of them, from villages to the regional capital.

Works Cited

Afkhami, Mahnaz and Erika Friedl. *Muslim Women and the Politics of Participation: Implementing the Beijing Platform.* New York: Syracuse University Press, 1997. Print.

Agarwal, Bina. "Structures of Patriarchy: The State, the Community and the Household." Indian Association for Women's Studies in *Two Steps Back? New Agricultural Policies in China and the Women Question* by Kelkar Govind. London, UK. Zed Books Ltd. 1988. Print

Al-Ali, Nadje Sadig. *Iraqi Women. Untold Stories from 1948 To The Present.* London: Zed Books Ltd., 2007. Print

Al-Ali, Nadje and Nicola Pratt. *Between Nationalism and Women's Rights: The Kurdish Women's Movement in Iraq.* Middle East Journal of Culture and Communication, Volume 4, Issue 3, pp 337-353. 2011. Print

―――― *What Kind of Liberation? Women and the Occupation of Iraq.* Berkeley: University of California Press, 2009. Print

Al-Khayyat, Sana. *Honour and Shame: Women in Modern Iraq.* London, British Library, 1990. Print.

American Bar Association. *Iraq Personal Status Law 1959.* Web. 12 Apr. 2013.

Amnesty International. *Trapped by Violence: Women in Iraq.* London, 2009.

Backer, Ralf and Ronald Ofteringer. "A Republic of Statelessness: Three Years of Humanitarian Intervention in Iraqi KRI of Iraq." *Middle East Report 187 – Humanitarian Intervention and North-South Politics in the 1990s.* 2004. Web. 13 Mar. 2013.

Ballington, Julie and Azza Karam. *Women in Parliament: Beyond Numbers.* Revised Edition. International Institute for Democracy and Electoral Assistance (IDEA), 2005.

Begikhani, Nazand. "Honour-based Violence among the Kurds: The Case of Iraqi KRI of Iraq." *'Honour': Crimes, Paradigms, and Violence against Women.* Eds. Lynn Welchman and Sara Hossain. London: Zed Books. 2005. 209 – 229. Print.

―――― "Kurdish Women and National Identity." Paper presented at the University of Exeter, April 2001 and Middle East Studies Association Meeting, October 2001. Web. 10 Apr. 2013.

Cook, Gretchen. "Role of Women in New Iraq of Concern." 22 Apr. 2003. Web. 27 Mar. 2013.

CSO/KRSO/UNFPA/PAN ARAB Project for Family Health. "Iraqi Women Integrated Social and Health Survey (I-WISH 2011)." 2012.

Dahlerup, Drude. *Women, Quotas and Politics*. New York Routledge Taylor and Francis Group, 2006. Print.

Dosky, Berivan. "My broken dream for Iraqi Kurdistan." *Guardian UK*. 17 Mar. 2013 Web. 10 Apr. 2013.

Gillespie, Paula, Neal Lerner. *The Allyn and Bacon Guide to Peer Tutoring*. Boston: Allyn, 2000. Print.

Gleick, James. *Chaos: Making a New Science*. New York: Penguin, 1987. Print.

Mahmoud, Houzan. "Human Chattel." *Guardian UK*. 2 May 2007. Web. 15 Apr. 2013.

Haghighat-Sordellini, Elhum. *Women in the Middle East and North Africa. Change and Continuity*. New York: Palgrave Macmillan, 2010. Print

Human Rights Watch. "Iraq." 2013. Web. 15 Feb. 2013.

Inter-Agency Information and Analysis Unit. "Iraq Information Portal." Web. 2 Apr. 2013.

Iraqi Al-Amal Association. *"Violence Against Women in Iraqi Kurdistan: A Field Research. 2001."* Web. 12 Apr. 2013.

———— *"Results of the Field Survey for Needs and Opinions of the Poor in Iraq"*. University of Bagdad. 2008. Web. 12 Apr. 2013

Iraq Independent High Electoral Commission (IHEC). "Regulation No. 3." *Iraq: Regulations for the Kurdistan Region Elections*. Web.

Inter-Parliamentary Union. *Informing Democracy: Building Capacity to Meet Parliamentarian's Information and Knowledge Needs*. 2009. France. Reports and Documents No. 59. Web. 10 Apr. 2013.

———— "Council of Representatives of Iraq." Web. 2 Apr. 2013.

Integrated Regional Information Networks. "Iraq: Honour Killings' Persist in Kurdish North." 6 Dec. 2007. Web. 10 Apr. 2013.

———— "KRI of Iraq Aziz: Another Victim of Stoning." 6 Jun. 2008. Web. 12 Apr. 2013.

Jawad, A. Haifaa. *The Rights of Women in Islam: An Authentic Approach*. Great Britain: Macmillan Press Ltd., 1998. Print.

Kabeer, Naila. "Resources, Agency, Achievements: Reflections on the Measurement of Women's Empowerment." *Development and Change*, Vol. 30, Issue 3, p. 435-464. 1999.

Kandiyoti, Deniz. *Women, Islam and the State*. Philadelphia: Temple University Press, 1991. Print

Kurdistan Democratic Party. "Kurdistan Women Union (KWU)." Web. 4 Apr. 2013.

Kurdistan Parliament. "Draft Constitution of Iraqi Kurdistan." Web. 17 Feb. 2013.

Kurdish Women Right's Watch. "Action Against Honor Killing." Web. 13 Feb. 2013.

Lichter, Ida. *Muslim Women Reformers: Inspiring Voices Against Oppression.* New York: Prometheus Books, 2009. Print

Margolies Beitler, Ruth and Angelica R. Martinez. *Women's Roles in the Middle East and North Africa.* California: Greenwood, 2010. Print

Maier, Sylvia. "Lifting the Veil in the Middle East – Editorials & Commentary – International Herald Tribune." *New York Times.* 19 Jun. 2006. Web. 10 Feb. 2013.

Martineau Nicolas-Guillaume. *The Decline in High-intensity Participation: A Model of Party Activism and Special-interest Influence on Policy.* Institut D'economie Publique. 2010.

McDowall, David. *A Modern History of the Kurds.* London: I.B.Tauris & Co Ltd., 2000. Print

Ministry of Higher Education and Scientific Research. "Studying for Master's degree in Kurdistan Region." 2010. Web. 24 Apr. 2013.

Moghadam, Valentine M. "The Middle East and North Africa: Social Change and Women's Rights." *Women and Politics Around the World: A Comparative History and Survey.* Eds. Joyce Gelb and Marian Lief Palley. California: ABC-CLIO, Inc., 2009. Print.

———— *Patriarchy and Economic Development. Women's Positions at the End of the Twentieth Century.* Oxford: Clarendon Press, 1996.

Mojab, Shahrzad. *Women Of A Non-State Nation, The Kurds.* California: Mazda Publishers, Inc., 2001. Print.

———— "No 'Safe Haven': Violence against Women in Iraqi Kurdistan". *Sites of Violence: Gender and Conflict Zones.* Eds. Wenona Giles and Jennifer Mary Hyndman. Berkeley: University of California Press, 2004. 108 – 133. Print

Muhsen, Abdulaziz. *Divorcement of Women in Research.* Duhok Institute for General Culture. 2011. Translated from Kurdish to English 2013. Print

Natali, Denise. *The Kurdish Quasi-State.* Syracuse: Syracuse University Press, 2010. Print

Noga, Efrati. *Women in Iraq: Past meets Present.* New York: Columbia University Press. 2012. Print.

Office of the High Commissioner for Human Rights. "Universal Declaration of Human Rights." *United Nations.* 2013. Web. 24 Feb. 2013.

Price, Joshua M. *Structural Violence: Hidden Brutality in the Lives of Women.* Albany: State University of New York Press, 2012.

Sabbagh, Amal. "Case Study: The Arab States: Enhancing Women's Political Participation." *Women in Parliament: Beyond Numbers.* Eds. Julie Ballington and Azza Karam. International Institute for Democracy and Electoral Assistance (IDEA), 2005.

True, Jasqui. *The Political Economy of Violence Against Women.* Oxford: Oxford University Press, 2012. Print.

UN Women. "United Nations Fourth World Conference on Women: Platform for Action." 1995. Web. 14 Jan. 2013.

United Nations. *The Convention on the Elimination of All Form of Discrimination Against Women and its Optional Protocol: Handbook for Parliamentarians.* Switzerland: United Nations, 2003, Print.

United Nations. "UN Assistance Mission for Iraq." Web 30 Apr. 2013.

Walby, Sylvia. "The 'Declining Significance' or the 'Changing Forms' of Patriarchy?" *Patriarchy and Economic Development. Women's Positions at the End of the Twentieth Century.* Ed. Valentine M. Moghadam. Oxford: Clarendon Press, 1996. 20-55. Print.

Whiteley, Paul and Patrick Seyd. *High-intensity Participation: the Dynamics of Party Activism In Britain.* Ann Arbor: The University of Michigan Press, 2002. Print.

World Bank. "Iraq Overview." Web. 2 Apr. 2013.

Yadav, Stacey Philbrick. "Does a Vote Equal a Voice?" *Middle East Research and Information Project.* Volume: 39, Fall 2009.

United Nations Development Program. "Women Economic Empowerment – Integrating Women into the Iraqi Economy." 2012. Web. 23 April 2013.

UNESCO at l'Iraq. "UNESCO and Education in IRAQ Fact Sheet." 28 March 2003. Web. 23 April 2013

116

Glossary

connectors: the systems, institutions, values, interests, and cultural norms that connect people across lines of conflict

cultural violence: the legitimization of violence in cultural institutions, such as religion, language, art, media, law, and education, that makes violence acceptable in society

direct violence: the observable incidences of self-directed, interpersonal, or collective violence, including physical, verbal, or psychological acts and acts that inhibit or insult our basic needs and/or physical persons

dividers: the systems, institutions, values, interests, and cultural norms that divide people in society and have the capacity to exacerbate conflict and/or violent

Kurdistan Region of Iraq (KRI): the autonomous region of northern Iraq, composed of the Duhok, Erbil, and Sulaimani governorates, and bordering the rest of Iraq to the south, Iran to the east, Syria to the west, and Turkey to the west

Kurdistan Regional Government (KRG): the legal entity representing the autonomous Kurdistan Region of Iraq, as recognized in the 2005 Iraqi constitution

negative peace: the absence of direct violence

peacebuilding: action to identify and support structures which will strengthen and solidify peace in order to avoid a resort to violence and/or violent conflict

peacefulness: the degree of manifestation of peace; the term peacefulness is often used to acknowledge that the various forms of peace are dynamic concepts, often in flux, and rarely achieved as complete and constant

peace capacities: the existing and potential systems, institutions, and cultural norms that provide the building blocks of peace for societies in conflict

positive peace: freedom from all forms of violence in the context of a sustainable social system

resilience: the capacity of social systems for repair, renewal, adaptation, and the absorption of stress without resort to violence or violent conflict

structural peace: a state of positive peace embedded in and supported by society's attitudes, institutions, and structures

structural violence: the systemic ways in which a given social, cultural, or economic structure or institution harms people by preventing them from meeting their basic needs

A note on sources: The definitions included here are composites, synthesized from many sources and refined through study and practice. The types of peace and violence are significantly influenced by the work of Johan Galtung, and the concepts of connecters, dividers, and peace capacities come directly from Mary Anderson's text *Do No Harm*. Additionally, the nuances of various definitions have been influenced by the work of Jurgen Brauer and J.P. Dunne, Peter Brorsen, the Institute for Economics and Peace, and former UN Secretary General Boutros Boutros-Ghali, as well as the editors, authors, and researchers of this collection. For more information on fundamental peacebuilding concepts, please see the works generally cited below.

Anderson, Mary. *Do No Harm: How Aid Can Support Peace – or War.* Boulder, Co: Lynne Rienner Publishers, 1999. Print.

Brauer, Jurgen and J. P. Dunne. *Peace Economics: A Macroeconomic Primer for Violence-Afflicted States.* Washington, D.C.: United States Institute of Peace, 2012. Print.

Boutros-Ghali, Boutros. "An Agenda for Peace: Preventive Diplomacy, Peacemaking, and Peace-keeping." New York: United Nations, 1992.

Galtung, Johan. *Peace by Peaceful Means: Peace and Conflict, Development and Civlization.* London: Sage, 1996. Print.

———— "Violence, Peace, and Peace Research" *Journal of Peace Research*, 6.3 (1969): 167-191.

Institute for Economics and Peace (IEP). "Structures of Peace: Identifying What Leads to Peaceful Societies." Sydney, Australia, 2011. Print.

Institute for Economics and Peace (IEP). "2011 Discussion Paper: New Dimensions of Peace – Society, Economy, and the Media." Sydney, Australia, 2011. Print